NEW
TRICKS
FOR OLD
DOGS

Copyright © 2016 Gene Perret
All rights reserved.

Published by Familius LLC, www.familius.com

Familius books are available at special discounts for bulk purchases, whether for sales promotions or for family or corporate use. For more information, contact Familius Sales at
559-876-2170 or email orders@familius.com.

Library of Congress Cataloging-in-Publication Data
2015955942

Paperback ISBN 9781942934462
Ebook ISBN 9781944822002
Hardcover ISBN 9781944822019

Printed in the United States of America

Edited by Adam McLain
Cover design by David Miles
Book design by Brooke Jorden

10 9 8 7 6 5 4 3 2 1

First Edition

NEW TRICKS

FOR OLD DOGS

28

LAUGHABLE LESSONS FOR PEOPLE TOO
STIFF TO CHANGE ... OR BEND ... OR MOVE

GENE PERRET

Dedicated to my good friend and personal
self-help guru, Ed Hercer.

CONTENTS

"*Courage can overcome fear . . . almost as well as hiding under the bed.*"
—*Anonymous*

"*Those people who think they know everything are a great annoyance to those of us who do.*" —*Isaac Asimov*

"*We are all here on earth to help others; what on earth the others are here for, I don't know.*" —*John Foster Hall*

"*A conference is a gathering of important people who singly can do nothing but together can decide that nothing can be done.*" —*Fred Allen*

"*It takes twenty years to make an overnight success.*" —*Eddie Cantor*

"*It has become appallingly obvious that our technology has exceeded our humanity.*" —*Albert Einstein*

"*The only way to get rid of temptation is to yield to it . . . I can resist everything but temptation.*" —*Oscar Wilde*

"*He has no enemies, but is intensely disliked by his friends.*" —*Oscar Wilde*

"*No good decision was ever made in a swivel chair.*" —*George S. Patton Jr.*

"*What part of 'No' don't you understand?*" —*Anonymous*

"*Be yourself. Everyone else is already taken.*" —*Oscar Wilde*

INTRODUCTION

"Life is a moderately good play with a badly written third act."
—Truman Capote

S ome things get better with age. For instance, wine and . . . uh . . .
well, just wine. And even wine is suspect. Suppose you discover a bottle of wine that has been hidden in some abandoned cellar—not a wine cellar, just a cellar—for, let's say, two thousand years. The bottle is covered with cobwebs and dust, but the liquid is still liquid. You can open that bottle of ancient wine, but you shouldn't drink it. Or, at least, you should have someone you don't particularly care for drink it first.

We assume some things get better with age, but they really don't—like antiques. We all assume that the older an antique is, the more valuable it is. Yet when you see heirlooms displayed on those TV shows about collectibles or someone bringing a relic to a pawnshop, you hear things like "Yes, this is a fine example of prediluvian [I made that name up], hand-carved pottery. I would say this particular piece dates back to about 600 B.C. It's one of the most extraordinary pieces I've ever seen, and I thank you for bringing it in."

The person who brought it in begins to salivate and says, "Yeah, but . . . ?" All that person wants to know is: *What's it worth?*

Then the expert says, "Of course, it does have some conditioning problems, which will affect the value."

The person who owns it says, "Yeah, so . . . ?" She still just wants to know what it's worth.

The expert says, "You'll notice that there is some discoloration about the base and that there are multiple scratches on the surface."

The thing is over 2,600 years old. You're going to get a few scratches with 2,600 years of use. I'm only in my seventies and I have a little discoloration, too. The point is that you would think things get better with age, but they only get scratched and change their color.

This is neither an accusation nor a complaint. It's recognizing reality. Things change with age. George Burns used to say, "I can do anything at eighty that I could do when I was twenty. Which gives you an idea what terrible shape I was in when I was twenty." Bob Hope said, "I don't feel old. I don't feel anything until noon. Then it's time for my nap." These gentlemen knew what they were talking about, because they were telling jokes, singing, and dancing even after they celebrated their hundredth birthdays. Of course, they told their jokes a bit more slowly, sang a bit more softly, and danced a bit more carefully—and they also had a few minor scratches and some discoloration—but they didn't let their age stop them.

These people understood the effects of age. Some people don't. The ones who don't understand aging are the young. They've never experienced it, and they think they never will. However, that doesn't stop them from considering themselves experts in the field. They keep trying to tell the older folks how to enjoy being older.

"C'mon, Pop," they say. "Come to the movies with us. It'll be fun."

No, it'll be sitting in a seat staring at a screen. At home, I can sit in a seat and stare at anything I want to stare at. If I get tired while staring, I can close my eyes, take a nap, and not worry about what I missed on the screen.

"C'mon, Pop," they say. "Come bowling with us. It's fun."

No. It's not fun; it's bowling. It entails moving parts of my body that haven't moved that way in years and don't particularly want to move that way today. And tomorrow, when I try to get out of bed, those same body parts will get their revenge on me for what I put them through today. That's not fun.

Age is not a bad thing; it just has some nasty side effects. It used to take me fifteen minutes to drive to the local library. Now it takes me forty-five minutes. The library is still the same distance away, and the car gets me there just as fast. The car hasn't slowed down at all. However, you have to consider the fifteen-minute drive then add on the fifteen minutes it takes me to get into the car and the fifteen minutes it takes me to get out of the car once I get there. As a result, the portal-to-portal traveling time is forty-five minutes.

Age is like the elevator operator of life. You step in, and he closes the door. He moves the controls, and you go up. Then he opens the door and says, "Slim waist and full head of hair get off here." Then he closes the door and you move to the next floor. He announces, "OK, this is where memory gets off." The next time the doors open, he says, "OK. This is where good hearing gets off . . . I said, 'This is where good hearing gets off.'" And it goes on and on like that. You lose a little bit at each stop.

Of course, growing old is not always that blatant or definitive. Often, we don't even realize it's happening, but it is. Once, I went to play some basketball with my nephews. Perhaps I would dazzle them with my ball-handling skills and my dead-eye shooting. One of my relatives fed me the ball around the top of the key, and it seemed like a perfect time to drill a jump shot. Now, to make a jump shot, one has to jump. It's required. Otherwise, they would call it a "stand there and throw the ball up" shot. So to jump, you have to bend your knees and then spring up from that position, propelling yourself into the air so that you can release the ball before your opponent can jump up and block it. So I bent my knees. When I tried to spring up from that position, my knees didn't get the message. I just stayed in that flexed position, and the guy guarding me just took the ball away from me. It didn't dazzle anyone, and no one threw the ball to me for the rest of the game, which was OK with me.

Sometimes we don't have to resort to denial; our brain does it for us. Recently, I had new photos taken. That's an ordeal because you have to be charming for the camera. No one wants to look like a grouch in an official portrait. But for a grouch like me, it's hard to remain charming for that long.

The photographer posed me, checked the lighting, focused the camera, positioned my hands, and then told me to smile. I told him I was smiling.

He said, "Try to smile so that it looks like a smile."

I said, "I don't have a smile like that. This is the only smile I have."

He said, "Well, try to imitate someone else smiling."

He kept telling me to lift my chin, tilt my head to the left, pull my shoulders back, look to this side, look to that side. Anyway, I tried to do everything he told me and be as charming as possible for the remainder of the shoot.

Then when the pictures came back, they were of some little old man. Mickey Rooney? My grandpa? Who was this man in the picture? That couldn't possibly be me! Could it? But it was.

Another time I realized my mind and body weren't on the same page was recently while I was playing golf. I was on the first tee and wanted to hit the ball about 260 yards down the fairway. My mind told my body exactly what to do. It said, *Take the club back with a full shoulder turn. This will coil your muscles so that you can release and swing through the ball with good control but full power.* I visualized it, and I even heard sounds as I swung. I heard *Whooooosh . . . whack . . . zoom.*

Well, my body didn't listen to a thing my mind said. It didn't take the club back with a full body turn. It just kind of went back a little bit and then hit the ball a little bit. It didn't go *Whooooosh . . . whack . . . zoom.* It sounded more like *Oooomph . . . blip . . . flop.* The ball traveled about 26 yards. For those of you who don't know much about golf, 26 yards is not as far as 260 yards. What made matters worse was that immediately after that shot, all my playing partners shouted out, "Great shot!"

All of us could talk to our bodies and visualize our golf swing as much as we wanted. The reality was that 26 yards was as far as any of us could hit it.

The point is that what was once a glorious jump shot is now just a "hold the ball out so the other team can take it away" shot. What used to be a charming and handsome young man smiling beguilingly into the lens is now a picture of a geezer. What once was a fierce, athletic 260-yard drive is now a painful, hopeless 26-yard dribble along the grass. Why? Because we're older now. Maybe wiser, but definitely older.

Now, the same thing happens with self-help advice. Self-help is wonderful. It has given confidence to the insecure. It has made fortunes for many. It has inspired many to earn great wealth, become fantastic leaders, and reach the pinnacles of fame on stage and screen. But after a certain age, it becomes impractical. It's great for the young who have the energy and the perseverance to apply it and benefit from it. For others, it must be tempered with common sense and reality. The jump shot is an effective tool for a young, athletic, skilled ballplayer. For the geezer, it's no longer in the repertoire.

So do we abandon self-help principles totally? Do we demean them and label them as ineffective and useless? Not at all. We adjust. Our minds may be dimmer and our bodies frailer, but to compensate, we have wisdom. We have gathered enough wisdom over the years to recognize that the self-help advice that most authors offer is not wise at all—at least, not for us. We've become sage enough to say to those authors, "Look, I wasn't smart enough to pay attention to what you were saying when I was young; I'm certainly not going to follow your advice now that I'm older and have an excuse not to do what you say."

We're smart enough to know that the self-help policies are designed for the young, but we're also intelligent enough to know that we can readjust those principles to suit our age. The game of golf is a fine example. As we hackers get older, we don't hit the ball as far. So what do we do? We take the place where we're going to hit the ball from and move it closer to where we're going to hit the ball to. Now we geezers don't have to hit the ball as far. We just create new tee boxes. The good golfers hit from the "blues." Those are the blue tees that the professional golfers hit from. We also have the "whites," where the average golfers hit from. Today, we've added the "reds," the "yellows," the "grays," and so on. Pretty clever adjustment, right?

And the professional golfers have adjusted as well. When they started getting on in years, they could no longer compete with the young studs. Some of them used to win a lot of money, but now they can't. So they created the "Champions Tour." That's a series of tournaments that older golfers—and only older golfers—can play in. Now they can win and collect prize money again because the younger guys who can beat them are not allowed to compete against them. Wonderful adjustment.

That's what this book is all about. It's a process of adapting the good, solid advice from self-help authors and tweaking it so that it now applies to us more senior citizens. The motto used to be years ago: "If you can't beat 'em, join 'em." We're changing that to "If you can't beat 'em, outsmart 'em."

So read on, and keep the advice of George Burns in mind: "You can't help getting older, but you don't have to get old."

CHAPTER ONE

DECIDE WHAT YOU WANT TO DO

"If you don't know where you're going, you might
wind up someplace else." —Yogi Berra

The first principle of most success-oriented literature is that to get what you want, you must decide what you want. It seems to make sense. Otherwise, once you get it, how will you know you got it? Even Napoleon Hill, the granddaddy of all self-improvement authors, states in the very first chapter of his classic book, *Think and Grow Rich,* that success demands a "definiteness of purpose." In other words, make up your mind. Decide what you want.

This is fine advice for youngsters in elementary, middle, or high school. Yes, they should be thinking about what they want to do with the rest of their lives. In fact, when I was a freshman in high school, the school counselors gave us a test to help us determine an appropriate life choice. It was based, supposedly, on our skills and our likes and dislikes. Many of the questions were oddly specific multiple-choice scenarios, like the following:

If you were in a room with a piano, would you . . .

   a. play the piano?
   b. fix the piano?
   c. paint the piano?

At the time, I didn't know how to play the piano, so I ruled out the first option immediately. I certainly didn't know how to fix a piano. In fact, I had no way of knowing whether this particular piano was broken or not. I had no paintbrush with me, so I couldn't paint the instrument either. So rather than select one of the listed choices, I wrote that I would go into another room that didn't have a piano.

I thought the question was stupid; I also thought my answer was appropriate. The school authorities felt just the opposite: their question was apropos; my answer was idiotic.

They had another dumb question that asked: "If someone gave you a glass of juice that was filled to only about the middle, would you consider that glass half empty or half full?" I wrote down that I would consider using a smaller glass. The school personnel had the same opinion about that response as they did about my previous one.

They weren't crazy about too many of my solutions to their questions. When one counselor spoke with me about the results of my test and which career choice those results indicated, she told me I should consider manual labor, janitorial work, or become a pirate.

As a consequence, I still had no idea what I really wanted to do, and the school authorities decided to wash their hands of the entire affair.

One advantage of us more mature self-helpers is that through the years, we've been able to gather data to test some of the various self-help precepts. We've noticed a flaw in the idea of ensuring your success by deciding exactly what you want. The flaw is that it doesn't work. Here's a test that you can quickly take to reinforce this conclusion in your own mind. Think of several of your friends. Now think of what they do for a living. Now, in your mind, honestly consider whether this is something that they have wanted to do since their youth. Or is it simply where they wound up? As Allen Saunders once said, "Life is what happens to us while we are making other plans."

One of the friends I thought about works in a dry goods store. People select bolts of fabric, and he runs it along a yardstick fastened to the counter and measures out the exact number of yards they want to purchase. It's an honorable occupation, and it provides for him and his family. However, I can't imagine that as a youngster he fell asleep at night dreaming about sliding out three yards of lavender-colored silk then taking a pair of scissors and adroitly cutting it to that exact length. It's hard to conceive that he would say to himself, "I'm determined to keep my grades up so that I can get admitted to a fine university where I can major in cloth measuring."

When he and the other kids would have been playing make-believe, one kid would say, "I want to be Gene Autry," another would shout, "I'll be Roy Rogers," and one of the girls would volunteer, "I'll be Annie Oakley, the greatest sharpshooter in the world." Our youngster in question would then say, "Good. And I'll be the guy who has a store in town that sells you all the fine materials to make your cowboy outfits."

I don't think that scenario ever happened.

Measuring cloth never was his *definite life's goal*. It was just a job that opened up, he interviewed for, and he got.

Isn't that true of a majority of the friends you listed? Isn't it an indication that knowing what you want in life doesn't guarantee that that's what you'll get in life?

There are several reasons for this:

Most of us want something, but we don't know what.

Ask any number of people on the street, "What do you want out of life?" and 90 percent of them will give you the same answer: "What?" Most of them don't have time to figure out what it is they want; they're too busy chasing after it.

Of course, many will offer the stereotypical quests: money, fame, or power. They just haven't taken the time to figure out what they're going to do to earn the money, what attributes they should develop to capture fame, or who or what they will have power over. Comedian Lily Tomlin joked, "I always wanted to be somebody, but now I realize I should have been more specific." The ladies who enter the Miss America Pageant all know what they want. They want to use their beauty, talent, and personality to create world peace. They've been espousing that cause from the original pageant in 1921 until today. So far, not one of them has succeeded.

So, again, we older folks have concluded that it probably is a good idea to decide what you want out of life. Practically, though, it doesn't do much good, because no one bothers to do it. We've also observed that there comes a point in your life when if you don't yet know what you want to be, you probably aren't going to be it.

We're determined to get exactly what we want—until we want something else more.

Even those of us who do take the time to think about a particular goal, plan for it, and devote ourselves to pursuing it can be easily dissuaded and change our minds. To test this conclusion, you don't even have to think of your friends; just review your own life.

My first specific goal, like most of my peers, was to be a cowboy. I idolized cowboys. They could ride and rope, they could fight and shoot, and they could sing. Not only could they sing, but they could sing while riding a horse. Even better than that, they could yodel. Of course, when you're singing while riding a horse, yodeling is not something you *do*. It just sort of happens. Nevertheless, they could yodel, and I wanted to be one of them.

Also, as a cowboy hero, I would be entitled to one sidekick. The sidekick was usually a clumsy guy who was not too smart and usually said things that people laughed at. I knew I was predestined to be a cowboy hero because I had lots of classmates who were eminently qualified for sidekickery.

I knew it would be difficult, but it was my definite goal in life. When I told my mom, she said, "Your father and I were hoping you'd be a doctor." I thought that was a silly goal. There were no Saturday matinees about doctors. No, for me it was either a cowboy hero or Tarzan. Since I'd had one or two bouts with poison ivy as a kid, Tarzan was out. Cowboy hero it was.

When I told my dad, he said, "There's not much money in it."

Then that ambition disappeared. It was replaced by becoming the champion of the world in boxing. Every boxer I had ever seen had fame, fortune, and gorgeous women—all the things an eleven-year-old child could want in life. I joined the Police Athletic League to begin my quest as the world's greatest boxer of all time. The first punch I got hit with ended that pursuit.

Various other dreams followed: all-American football player, famous movie star, powerful politician . . . many came and went.

So as I grew older, I learned that you not only have to know what you want in life but also for how long you're going to want it.

We definitely want what other people tell us we want.

Many people don't really want what they want in life. They want what other people want them to want. We tend to pursue the goals that our parents want us to pursue (and are willing to pay for). Sometimes, we want what public opinion or tradition tells us we want.

One gentleman I knew was a doctor. Becoming a doctor is a considerable commitment. Your grades have to be good. You must be accepted into a respectable pre-med program. You have to study for several years during medical school and then perhaps for a few more years in your specialty. Working through your internship is not easy. But at the end of all this sacrifice and struggle is the title "Doctor." This gentleman earned that title.

His parents were justifiably proud of him. He earned another title besides "Doctor." It was "My son, the doctor."

He opened his practice, treated patients, and spent most of his time working on the screenplay that he wanted to write and sell. Now that he had successfully followed someone else's dream, he was prepared to pursue his real goal in life.

Another friend of mine who lived in the Northeast received a wonderful job offer. To accept it, though, he had to move to Southern California. He was not only willing to make the move but also thrilled at the wonderful career opportunity it presented. He told his family about it, expecting them to be excited for him. They weren't. His older brother said, "We'll never get to see you anymore. We won't be able to go to the Philadelphia Eagles games together anymore."

My friend said to his brother, "You can come visit me in California."

His brother said, "I can't afford that kind of travel."

My friend said, "I can come back and visit."

His brother said, "Yeah, you say that, but you won't."

The brother argued and cajoled. Finally, he convinced my friend that even though the job offer paid well and would be an excellent career boost, it was not worth separating brothers who enjoyed each other's company.

Following the wants and desires of his family, my friend turned down the offer. Two months later, his brother moved to Florida.

We old geezers can have naps but not dreams.

People are tolerant of young people who have glorious dreams. We older folks who declare a definite goal in life must prepare to be bombarded with ridicule. The world believes that young folks can achieve a lofty goal but old fogies can't.

Have you ever had one of those mornings when the sun seems brighter, the air smells fresher, and colors are more vibrant? I had one of those mornings recently. I skipped down to breakfast full of enthusiasm, knowing all was right with the world. It was glorious.

I proclaimed to my spouse, "I'm going to make my fortune."

She said, "For a man in his dotage, that's commendable."

Well, almost all was right with the world, but I didn't let her negativity deter me.

"I'm going to find the Lost Dutchman's Mine," I announced.

She was unimpressed. "And where is the Lost Dutchman's Mine?" she asked.

I didn't fall for her trick. "No one knows exactly where it is. If they did, it wouldn't be lost, would it? But it's hidden somewhere in the Superstition Mountains of Arizona."

She said, "So are the bleached bones of a lot of the people who tried to find it."

I said, "Good. Less competition."

"Where'd you get this idea?" she asked.

"I watched a documentary on TV about the lost fortune, and all during the show I kept hearing *You're the one who's going to find it . . . you're the one who's going to find it.* It was like the Dutchman himself was talking to me."

My wife was still unimpressed. "All during his life, he never talked. Now that he's dead, he has a chat with you."

"Look, Honey," I said, "I have this feeling. This lost gold mine is just sitting out there, and if I can find it, we'll be rich. You'll have a maid to do the dishes. We'll go everywhere by chauffeur-driven limousine."

"Which brings up an interesting point," she said. "How much is this going to cost?"

I said, "Not much. Maybe a few supplies, that's all."

She said, "Well, you're going to need at least one other jackass."

(Notice the thinly veiled ridicule received when we older citizens proclaim a goal.)

She then asked, "Do you know anything about gold?"

"Not much," I admitted, "but I've always been fond of it."

"Do you know how to spot it in the ground?"

I said, "Not exactly."

She said, "Do you know how to mine it, load it into carts, and bring it to the surface?"

"Not really."

"Do you know that no rich gold deposits have ever been found in the Superstition Mountains? Naturalists, engineers, and geologists all agree that it's an unlikely location for gold."

I said, "C'mon. What do they know?"

She said, "You're determined, aren't you?"

I said, "Honey, it's a dream, a fantasy. It's a gamble, sure, but every once in a while, a man has to chase a rainbow."

"Go chase your dream," she said. "But try to keep the costs down. We can't afford to waste money."

I was delighted and eager to get things underway. I showered, dressed, and was ready to go shopping for a few essentials when I realized I was missing something. "Honey," I said, "where are my tennis shoes?"

She said, "In the family room where you took them off."

There they were.

"Have you seen my hat?" I asked.

"It's in the hall closet."

"How about my jacket?"

She said, "It's here in the kitchen draped over the back of your chair."

"Thanks," I said. I kissed her and rushed out the back door.

I came back in.

Without me even asking, my wife said, "Your car keys are on the credenza in the foyer."

I picked them up and started out the door again. I heard my wife mutter to herself, "Rest in peace, Dutchman. Your secret is safe."

So be prepared for ridicule.

Sadly, the advice to know what you want to do emphasizes the wrong concepts. "Knowing" can be important (if you can manage it). "Wanting" is significant also (although, as we've seen, it can change). But the key word in the admonition is "you." *You* have to know. *You* have to want. *You* are the key factor.

So was Napoleon Hill wrong? Should we not decide on a dream? Should we not devote our energies to pursuing it? Of course he wasn't wrong. Yes, we should have a dream that we want to pursue, but we do have to decide and act when we're young enough to produce results.

A world-class tennis player once stated, "It takes at least five years to become a good tennis player, and it takes more than fifteen years to become a world-class tournament player." So I decided then and there on my goal in the sport. I would devote the rest of my life to becoming a mediocre or less-than-mediocre tennis player. I succeeded almost immediately. I've been resting on my non-laurels ever since.

CHAPTER TWO

DESIRE IS THE KEY TO ACHIEVEMENT

"Boredom: the desire for desires." —Leo Tolstoy

A young husband enters his house and shouts, "Hi, Honey! I'm home."

His beautiful wife eagerly greets him with a hug and a kiss and says, "Darling, how was your day?"

"It was wonderful," he replies. "I think I'm making an impression on my manager, and I have several projects that seem quite promising."

"That's lovely. But you must be exhausted. Sit down and relax. May I make you a refreshing cocktail?"

"No, you may not."

Taken aback, she says, "What?"

He repeats, "No, you may not make me a cocktail."

She asks, "But why?"

"Because tonight I'm taking you out for a gourmet dinner. I've made reservations for just us two at the Café de Lah-De-Dah."

"But, Sweetheart, that's so expensive."

He draws her closer. "Having dinner with my favorite girl is worth every penny."

"And it's so far away. Aren't you too tired to drive after working so hard all day?"

"Not at all. With you beside me, the time will go quickly."

"I'll have to change and put on some makeup."

"Yes, do," he says. "And wear that stunning red dress of yours. That always excites me so."

"My, my, you seem so romantic tonight."

"I'm very romantic. In fact, after dinner, we'll stop at the Starlight Ballroom and dance the night away."

She says, "Are you sure you're ready for all this activity? You'll be exhausted when you get home."

He says, "Not too exhausted, my dear, if you catch my drift."

She giggles and rushes off to prepare for an exciting and romantic evening.

Picture the same couple after several decades of marriage.

He enters the house. "I'm home."

She says, "Yeah, I know."

He says, "You wanna go out for dinner?"

She says, "OK."

He says, "Where do you want to go?"

She says, "Someplace where we don't have to get dressed up."

Do you notice how the desire has dwindled as the years have gone by? And it's not just romance; it happens with lots of things. After a good round of golf, a young player might say, "That was great. Let's have some lunch and maybe we can play another nine. Whaddya say?"

A guy who's been hacking around the course for many years tees off on the fourth hole, turns to his playing partners, and says, "How many more holes do we have to go?"

It even happens in church. A man bows his head in prayer, and his wife nudges him. He says, "What? I'm praying."

She says, "You were snoring."

It happens with many things you used to enjoy—for example, playing with the grandkids. A man's wife says, "Why don't we go to a movie?"

The man says, "I hate movies."

Another time, his wife says, "I volunteered to babysit today. Your grandchildren—Tommy, Susie, Martha, and Bobby—are coming over."

He says, "When will they be here?"

She says, "In about an hour."

He says, "Yeah, well, I'm going to the movies."

Our desires desert us as we age. That's why you can't teach an old dog new tricks. You can act as enthused as you want. You can pet and hug and baby-talk the critter all day. You can have your pockets loaded with scrumptious dog biscuits as rewards. Still, you can't teach an old dog new tricks. Why? Because the dog don't give a damn.

Remember when Trixie was a puppy? She would get excited, jump up and down exuberantly, drool ridiculously, and run around waiting for you to throw the ball. When you did toss it, she would gallop after it, pounce on it, and maybe miss picking it up on the first or second try because she was overeager. When she finally gripped it firmly with her teeth, she'd race back to you so she could be fawned over and loved. Then you'd both repeat the process over and over again.

That was then, and this is now:

Trixie just lies there. She doesn't even lift her head off the ground. She simply raises her eyes upwards to look at you and says to herself, *What now? Oh no, not the dreaded tennis ball game again. We've been playing that pointless game for eleven years. I don't know whether he knows it or not, but that's seventy-seven years in a dog's life. Seventy-seven years, man. Enough already.*

Oh, look, now he's picking up the ball. I don't know how he can do that. It's covered with seventy-seven years of slobber. I don't even like to pick it up. And I'm a dog.

Look. Now he's pretending that he threw the ball. I'm not going for that fake-out anymore. I'm not even going to move my eyes in that direction. I'm just going to stare at him in disbelief. I stopped falling for that trick after the first four years. That's seven years ago, or forty-nine years of doggie time. Ah, he finally threw the ball. I suppose I should go after it. OK, but I'll tell you this: I'm not going to run.

So poor, weary Trixie reluctantly gets up and ambles toward the ball. Maybe "ambles" is even too strong a word. Strolls? Saunters? Moseys? That's it. Trixie *moseys* toward the ball. However, she doesn't pounce. She just stares at the ball, thinking: *If I pick it up, I've got to bring it back to him. When I do, he'll just throw it again. Maybe I should just pick it up and spit it into the yard next door. Let's see if he has enough ambition to climb over the fence and bring it back. Let him play fetch for a little while.*

This is the game of fetch once the desire has disappeared.

The second chapter of Napoleon Hill's classic, *Think and Grow Rich*, is entitled "Desire." The subtitle of that chapter tells us that desire is "The Starting Point of All Achievement." Desire is like a fire. It's the fire that burns within our soul. However, like all fires, it tends to burn down. Eventually, it reduces itself to glowing embers. Those embers won't drive Trixie to scoot after a tennis ball like a sprightly puppy, nor will they fuel our drive toward success.

A reporter once asked the late entertainer Sammy Davis Jr. what he would be doing if he weren't in show business. Sammy Davis responded (and I'm paraphrasing), "I have no idea. All I know is show business. Without it, I wouldn't be doing anything."

The self-help genre suggests that we should select our desire. Do we want to be a ballplayer, a ballet dancer, or a guy who makes animal figures out of balloons? Whatever we select, we should create a desire for that ambition. It would probably be more accurate to say that our desire selects us. It's not something that we implant in ourselves; it's something that is already there. Sammy Davis didn't choose to go into show business; he was *born* to entertain. In a sense, he had no choice. It's a fine distinction, but an important one.

Desire can't be manufactured. Sammy Davis could not have said, "Well, the show business thing doesn't seem to be working out, so I'll become a welder. That's it. I'll generate the desire to weld things together." No, the genuine desire was to sing, dance, and entertain. Anything else would have been a compromise. There could have been any number of alternate career choices, but there was only the one sincere desire.

If we abandon our original desire, what can replace it? We may try many things. One replacement might be bravado. We try to convince others that we are following our true quest when we really aren't. We adopt a new "desire" and try to convince the world that it is our true vocation. "Oh yes," we say, "I love my job, and my boss is a gem. He's an inspiration to me. I wouldn't change a thing even if I could." Meanwhile, we're trying to get our inspirational boss fired. The world is not fooled. More importantly, neither are we.

There's a story about a gentleman who hated his job. He was a daredevil who was forced to perform a dangerous feat. He would dive from a platform eighty feet high into a shallow kiddies' swimming pool with less than one foot of water in it. People flocked to see his performance. Upon his introduction, the man would climb up the seemingly endless ladder, step out onto the platform, and address the eager crowd.

"Ladies and gentlemen," he would begin, "I am about to dive headfirst off this elevated platform into a ridiculously shallow pool. This feat is exceedingly dangerous, probably impossible. Yet, I will do it for your entertainment—unless you decide that I shouldn't do it. If I do it, chances are that I will be maimed for life and possibly killed. My family will grieve. They will have no one to support them. They will suffer terribly. Yet I will do it if you so choose. I ask you now: should I do it or shouldn't I?"

The audience would be so moved that they would all shout, "No, don't do it! Don't jump!"

He would say, "Thank you all for allowing me this reprieve. I will not jump. But be sure to tell all your friends to be here for the eight o'clock show later tonight."

That's bravado. He doesn't want to make this dive, but he pretends for the moment that he does. It may fool the crowd, but it's not fooling him.

We could devote our energy and our efforts to someone else's desire. How many people are doctors today because it was something their parents demanded of them? How many people struggled through law school because Mom and Dad were footing the expenses? How many people are business executives because the traditional wisdom was that they should get a college degree, get a good job, and then work their way up the company hierarchy? It was genuine desire that motivated them but not necessarily their personal desire.

Sometimes we deceive ourselves. We settle on a desire that is not ours, and we diligently convince ourselves that it is. There's a story of a man who had a suit custom made by a terribly incompetent tailor. When he went to pick up his new suit, he tried it on only to find out that one pants leg was two inches longer than the other. The tailor said, "That's fine. All you have to do is, when you walk, you kind of limp a little. Pull this leg up so that it looks like the pants are perfect."

He tried on the jacket, and it was so tight around his middle that he could hardly button it. The tailor said, "When you put it on, just suck in your tummy, button the coat, and it'll look fine."

Of course, the right sleeve was shorter than the left one. The tailor advised: "Just pull this arm up into the sleeve, stretch the other arm out, and you'll look wonderful."

So the man followed all the instructions, and when people saw him wearing the suit, they all asked for the name of his tailor. The man asked why they wanted to go to his tailor. They said, "Any person that can fit a body as misshapen as yours has got to be an artist."

The man forced himself into a badly tailored outfit; we can likewise be tempted to squeeze ourselves into an ill-advised desire. Both devices are foolish.

Our task is not to create a desire but to cooperate with the desire that is already within.

So what do we do if we agree that we can't select our desires, we can't manufacture our desires, and we can't replace genuine desire but we realize that the desire we used to have at one time has now burned down to semi-hot embers or perhaps even cold ashes? It's simple: we admit it. We accept the fact that what once thrilled us no longer thrills us. But isn't that surrendering? Isn't that giving up? Isn't that confessing that we can no longer cut the mustard? Yes, it is.

And what's wrong with that?

We can't select our desires. So why try? We can study ourselves (as we did when we were younger), investigate (as we did when we were younger), and discover what our present desire really is (as we should have done when we were younger).

Amazing. We now have a new plan for our lives. It's a plan that is consistent not only with the sage advice of many self-helpers but also with our energy level and age bracket. If we're honest, it should serve us well.

Let's return to the example of our favorite dog, Trixie. She has decided with her canine wisdom that playing fetch with a sloppy tennis ball is no longer the thrill it once was. She's retired from that activity, except perhaps for occasional "Old-Timer Games" and special events. But, again, using her canine sagacity, she's discovered a new activity that she thoroughly enjoys. It's become her new definite and primary desire. It is to nap.

So now, when her master prompts her to fetch, she thinks, *No, thank you. I prefer to lie here in the sun, warm up my tired bones, and rest and relax. I desire a nap.*

When the master tries to cajole her with "C'mon, girl. C'mon on over here and see me," she responds, *No, I want to nap. And I want to nap right here. Not there; here. If you want to pet me and make a fuss, you'll have to come over here—to where I'm napping—and do it. No, no, no—don't bring the ball!*

CHAPTER THREE

SETTING GOALS

"How can you make sure you never miss your target? Shoot first. Whatever you hit, call that your target." —Anonymous

magine a football field with no stripes on it. It has no yard markers. It has no hash marks. It has no logo at midfield. It's a blank sheet of green grass. A game played on such a field would be chaos. Neither of the teams would know where they were. Ironically, that wouldn't matter, because they also wouldn't know where they were going. In a normal football game (one with the traditional white stripes on the field), each team would drive towards the opponent's goal line. Cross that line, and you're awarded six points. On a blank field, though, there is no goal line. Theoretically, you could begin a game like this in Philadelphia and, if one team is dramatically more talented than the other, the game could continue through Pittsburgh. Of course, if the more skilled team were going in the other direction, the game could wind up in the Atlantic Ocean. In short, you need a goal. You need a goal line.

Young children realize this when they play a game of street football. The first thing they do is establish the goal lines. "OK, that lamppost down there is the goal line. And at the other end, the back of Mr. O'Malley's Ford station wagon is the other goal line." They establish order. They have targets to shoot for to score points.

Of course, if Mr. O'Malley comes out of his house, starts his car, and drives off, what then? If none of the players notice his departure, it could be that one of the goal lines is now traveling somewhere along the Schuylkill Expressway. However, we'll let the Street Football Rules Committee make a ruling on that.

The kids would probably be able to handle the problem themselves. They'd say, "OK, the puddle of oil under where Mr. O'Malley's station wagon used to be is now the goal line."

Goals are important. If you doubt that, watch a professional football game on television. A player ambles down the field, avoids one tackler, is hit at around the five-yard line, and falls forward into the end zone. The referee raises his hands, signaling a touchdown.

But is it a touchdown? Not yet. Now the referee faces the TV camera and announces, "The previous play is under review." That means they're going to show the alleged touchdown about forty more times from about six different angles. The announcers will analyze the play for you.

The rules state that if the player is in full possession of the ball, and any part of that ball crosses the goal line before that player touches the ground with any part of his body besides his hands or feet, that player is deemed to have scored a touchdown.

So you look at the play again . . . in slow motion. One announcer suggests, "It appears from this angle that his knee touched the ground a yard short of the goal line." His sidekick says, "Yes, but it's the position of the ball that determines the score. Was the ball over the goal line when his knee touched the ground?"

They show the play again from a different angle. "Well, from this point of view, it's hard to tell," one announcer says.

The other says, "But his knee is definitely on the ground."

The other insists, "But where is the ball?"

They bring up another view of the play . . . in slow motion, again. The commentator says, "The ball is definitely across the goal."

The first one then asks, "Yes, but where is his knee?"

This back-and-forth continues through infinite replays in infinitely slow motion, and each announcer offers an infinite number of comments on the play. Did the ball cross the goal? Did the ball not cross the goal? I would suggest they all simply say "Close enough" and give them the six points.

But no. The goal line is that important. That's why the field needs white lines. A definite, clearly marked goal is essential. You can't just be close enough; you have to reach the goal. That's apparently axiomatic in football, and to self-helpers, it's paramount to success.

Goals, goals, goals, goals, goals. In football, it's a line. In hockey, it's a line, but it's also a net. In a footrace, it's a piece of tape. In ice-skating, it's jumping up, spinning around three times, and landing on your skates again. (Although sometimes the skaters who land on their bottoms—rather than their skates—get up and win the event anyway.)

We all have goals. We've had them all of our lives. In the early grades, it was getting a gold star glued to your collar. In middle school, it was coming home with a report card full of A's, some of them with plus marks after them. In high school, it was getting a date with the prettiest cheerleader. In college, often, it was just finding out where your classroom was.

When you joined the postcollege adult world, it was getting an entry-level position. Then it was becoming a supervisor. Then it was becoming a manager. Then becoming a vice president, then president, then retirement . . . and that brings us back to the now. That brings us back to this book.

Those of us who have lived through this litany of various goals are pretty much fed up with establishing them. But no, the self-helpers won't let us have a respite. We must establish more goals, new goals, and old-person goals. They feel that achievement is impossible without goals. Many of the dedicated self-helpers, in fact, feel that existence is impossible without goals. The saying goes, "You fail at 100 percent of the goals you don't set." Self-helpers say that's not trying. I call it a perfect record.

They also want our goals to be categorized. We must list short-term goals, mid-range goals, and long-term goals. How about this: my short-term goal is to take a nap; my long-term goal is to wake up from that nap.

The goals also must be lofty. The mantra of many of the self-help books is "to shoot for the stars." That way, even if you fall short, you're still up pretty high. They forget that if you shoot for the stars and fall short, you could go plummeting helplessly through space for the next millennium or two. You could become the next Halley's Comet.

Those of us with considerable experience realize that overly lofty goals can be an impediment. It can be quite traumatic to reach for too much. My mother had a quaint quip for that when I would order too many good things at a restaurant. When I couldn't clean my plate, she'd say, "Your eyes are bigger than your belly."

It may be wrong to create goals that are too demanding, too challenging, or even impossible to attain. Consider the tale of the *Geococcyx californianus* (pronounced "Geococcyx californianus"). You may know this animal better as the roadrunner. You may know it even better as the real-fast cartoon bird that keeps outsmarting Wile E. Coyote and keeps saying "Beep-beep." A recent article I read said that the roadrunner is a flightless bird. That's sad. This poor creature has a goal of flying. It wants to fly, but it can't. It must be humiliating.

Most other birds fly. Well, except the ostrich, which doesn't really look like a bird. It looks like a ball of feathers with legs and its head stuck in the sand. Naturally, that wouldn't fly. If it tried to fly, it could tear its head off. Then, too, there's the penguin, which doesn't really look like a bird, either. It looks like a maître d'. Penguins live in the Antarctic, where there's no reason to fly. There are no trees to land in, no telephone wires to perch on . . . nothing but ice. If you take off and fly in the Antarctic, the only place to land is on the ground. Since the critter is already on the ground, why bother? It makes sense that penguins don't fly. And, of course, there's chicken. But on the whole, most birds fly.

But the roadrunner looks like a bird, so I always assumed it could fly. Although, come to think of it, I've never seen one in flight. Although, come to think of something else, I wouldn't recognize a roadrunner in the air, so I don't know if I've ever seen one in flight or not. But we can easily assume that it should fly. If it looks like a bird and acts like a bird, it should fly like a bird.

It's not unreasonable to expect certain things to fly. How would you like it if you rushed to the airport, boarded an aircraft, stuffed your luggage into the overhead compartment, fastened your seat belt, and returned your seat back to its fully upright and locked position, then heard the pilot's voice over the intercom: "Ladies and gentlemen, this is your captain speaking. Welcome aboard. This particular aircraft is a flightless aircraft. We'll be leaving the gate in about five minutes and will taxi all the way to Cleveland. If there's anything we can do to make your trip more enjoyable . . ."?

Yes, there is something you can do. You can *fly* this plane to Cleveland. This is an airplane; it should fly. If it can't fly, the airline should be dreadfully embarrassed.

The roadrunner is a bird; therefore, it should fly. It seems rather heartless that a bird that can't fly exists. Although it's probably better than a fish that can't swim. Is there such a thing as a swimless fish? If there were, it probably would have become extinct years ago.

Are there other anomalies in nature? Are there crawlless snakes? Quillless porcupines? Stinkless skunks? Are there octopuses that run out of ink? Who knows? The article didn't mention any of these. But it definitely did mention that the roadrunner is a flightless bird. This must be terribly frustrating and demoralizing for this bird to have a goal of flying but be incapable of flight. Does the roadrunner sometimes pause while scurrying around the desert floor, look up into the sky, watch the sparrows, cactus wrens, and hawks floating gracefully among the clouds, and say to herself, "I wish I could soar like a bird . . . wait a minute, I am a bird!"?

This is dangerous because it could lead to delusions of airworthiness. A particular roadrunner could perch upon some precipice (presumably having climbed up there) and, in a fit of self-esteem, thrust forward, spread its wings, and shout:

"Oh, yeah, I am a bird! . . . oh, no, I am a flightless b

                              i

                                i

                                i

                                  r

                                    r

                                  r

                                      r

                                      d ."

A similar crash landing could happen when we establish goals that are beyond our abilities. This was an epiphany for me. In learning about the frustration and mortification of the humble roadrunner, I realized the futility of lofty ambitions. I had to share this with my spouse, who always tries to goad me into superb achievements. As she puts it: "Why don't you try to do something?"

When she came in the room, I said to her, "This is absolutely amazing."

"What?"

"The roadrunner is a flightless bird."

"So?"

"So, it's very interesting."

"Oh?" she said in a tone that implied it wasn't really very interesting, except maybe to the easily interested.

"I think it's incredible that this bird has wings but it doesn't know how to fly."

"That's not so unbelievable. You have golf clubs."

I stared at her.

She went on. "You have a toolbox."

I was still speechless.

She continued. "You have a . . ."

"OK, OK," I said. "I get your point."

"Besides," she said, "I don't believe it."

I said, "It's right here in print." I showed her the article.

She said, "I still don't believe it."

She looked it up on her smartphone and quoted to me, "The roadrunner, noted among desert birds for killing snakes, is a fast, agile runner, but rarely flies."

Rarely flies.

That's a whole different story. It implies that the *Geococcyx californianus* can fly but just can't be bothered.

Eureka. Now this bird is truly my hero. Since this realization, I have established a new goal—to ignore the self-help pundits and become like the roadrunner. Yes, there are things I can do, but I'd rather not. And with that, I'm off for my nap. Beep-beep.

CHAPTER FOUR

PRIORITIZE AND ORGANIZE

"Organizing is what you do before you do something, so that when you do it, it's not all mixed up." —A. A. Milne

Self-helpers love order. They idolize a neat desk, an orderly notebook, and file cabinets in which you can actually find whatever it is you're looking for. They want, as my mom used to say, "a place for everything and everything in its place." They expect you to dream—and not only to dream but to dream big. Nothing is beyond your scope; you can have it all. You can do anything. However, they do demand that you do everything in proper sequence. You must prioritize.

You're allowed to have unlimited fantasies, but each fantasy must take its proper place in line. It's like going into a crowded delicatessen for ham on rye at lunch. You're hungry for something to eat, and you crave a ham on rye. The self-help advocates tell you that you're entitled to that ham on rye. If you want it, order it. But the deli insists that you pick a number and that you won't get your ham on rye until your number is called. You have pulled number 147 from the ticket dispenser, and the clerk behind the counter shouts, "Number 34." You must graciously and patiently wait for 112 other customers to place their orders before you can finally chomp down on your ham on rye.

That hardly feels like taking charge of your life, but it's orderly. And that's what this literature promotes. Yes, you're invited to pursue your dream, but you must first determine how you're going to do that. What is step A? What is step B? What is step C? You must plan a schedule. You have to make a list of your priorities.

You are expected to make a litany of short-term goals. You also need a prediction of long-term goals. What are you going to do today, and what do you plan to do ten years from now? My question is: if you don't get around to everything on today's to-do list, how will that affect those things that you've jotted down for ten years from now? Should you alter your ten-year plan now, or should you wait until you get to it and then break out the eraser or the Wite-Out?

Instead of being outside chasing rainbows, you're sitting at your desk writing interminable to-do lists. It's possible to design a working schedule for today but get so bogged down creating your ten-years-from-now forecasts that "today" has already morphed into "tomorrow." So you've got your priorities well planned, but you're already a day behind. You probably recognize this phenomenon from your school days—it would only be the second day of the new school year and already you were four weeks behind in your homework.

It's possible that years from now, someone could ask, "Are you a success?" and you could say, "Well, not yet. But I have a schedule here that says I will be."

Planning, scheduling, and organizing are wonderful for the young. They have unlimited time ahead of them for making unlimited lists. We of the older generation have limited time available. Do we really want to spend it jotting down list after list after list . . . after list . . . and so on?

My priorities are simple. As I mentioned earlier, my short-term goal is to take a nap. My long-term goal is to wake up from the nap. I don't even have to write that down—I've got it memorized.

Thanks to the constant prodding of self-helpers, I've grown to hate lists. I detest them; I despise them. Not my own—I never write lists—but my wife's. I've traveled all over the world. I've taken plane, train, and car trips and survived them all without having to make any lists. When my wife, though, is going out of town, she always makes a giant list . . . for me. When she last gave me a list, our conversation went a little like this:

"I don't need a list," I assured her.

"I'd feel better if we went over this list together," she said.

"I'm a grown man," I said.

"I know that," she said. "That's why I've made a long list."

"Sweetheart, when I go on a journey, I don't write out a set of instructions, do I?"

She said, "That's because when you go away, you leave a responsible, dependable person here to take care of things."

"Right."

She said, "I don't have that luxury. All I have is you."

She started with a detailed list of directions for watering the houseplants.

I said, "Honey, I'm a fairly successful businessman. I have over 250 people under my supervision."

"Yes, but they all water themselves. If they didn't, you'd have 250 employees drawing medical benefits because most of them would be suffering from dry rot."

She had a point, so we went over the detailed list, and I nodded that I understood each item and would execute all of them faithfully.

She harrumphed. I hate when spouses harrumph—especially when they have good reason to.

"Now let's talk about the dog," my wife said.

I laughed again. I said, "This is ironic. You have three quarters of a page on how, what, and when to feed the mutt but not one sentence on how to feed me."

She said, "The dog can't whip out a credit card and go to a nearby restaurant."

Again, she had a point.

"Should we have a quick trial run?" she asked.

"What is this? The Department of Motor Vehicles, where I have to pass a test to stay home alone? I know how to feed a dog."

"I just want to be very explicit, because the last time I went away, it cost a fortune to feed the puppy."

"What are you talking about?" I asked.

She said, "The $11.26 long-distance phone call asking where we keep the can opener."

I said, "I never called and asked you that."

She said, "The dog did."

"Very funny," I said. "Now why don't you just tell me exactly where the can opener is."

She said, "I wrote that on the list, but it's in the top drawer in the kitchen right next to the sink."

"To put your mind at ease, I do know where the kitchen and the sink are."

She said, "Of course you do. That's where you store all your dirty dishes and silverware until my return."

I said, "You know, I thought I was going to miss you, but you're taking care of that nicely."

"Just be sure to bring in the newspaper and the mail each morning. It's on the list."

"No, I thought I'd get an easy chair and sit out on the lawn and read them rather than lug them all the way into the house."

She said, "Just remember to do it."

"I will."

She said, "I'm going to call you every night to make sure you're following everything on the list."

I said, "Fine. If 911 answers, hang up."

She harrumphed again. I hated it again.

I said, "C'mon, I'll get the car loaded for you." I picked up her luggage, carried it out to the driveway, and loaded it into the trunk of the car.

"Have you got everything you need?" I asked.

Another harrumph.

"Well, I was just checking," I said.

She slipped in behind the steering wheel and I said, "I have some in-structions for you, too."

"Oh really? What are they?"

I said, "Have a good time, and don't worry about anything here."

She said, "I will, and I'll try."

Then she drove off.

I missed her even before she made the right-hand turn at the corner of our street. I watched as the car disappeared, and I wished that she were here with me now. I wanted her here not just because she's a caring, con-siderate, and efficient wife, and not just because she's got a great sense of humor and is fun to be with; I missed her for all those reasons, but mostly I missed her because I realized I had locked myself out of the house.

The exhaustive list didn't prevent me from locking myself out of my abode, and it certainly didn't help me get in once I found out I was locked out. In fact, I find short-term lists to be generally useless. You don't have to jot down what you're going to do today. You're here; just do it. You don't need a cheat sheet. And the ten-year plan is worthless, too. Ten years is a long way off. (Well, it's ten years off, to be exact.) Of course, if you insist on mapping out your activities and accomplishments for a decade from now, you should definitely jot those down. There is no way that ten years from now you'll remember all those things. That especially applies to us older self-improvers.

I'm sure you've had the same strange experiences I've had. You're sitting comfortably on the couch when suddenly you realize you have something urgent to do. Reluctantly, you get up from the couch and go into another room—the room where you have to be to do whatever it was that you realized you suddenly have to do. However, once you get in that room, you have no idea why you're there. You do recall that it was something terribly urgent. Why else would you get up off of a comfortable couch if it weren't urgent? But you can't for the life of you remember what it was. The harder you try to think of why you came into this room, the more it escapes you. Finally, you surrender, go back into the first room, and sit back down on the couch. When you're about two-thirds seated, you remember what it was you wanted to do.

Now the question is: Do you get up again to do it? Absolutely not. You already tried to do it once, and you failed. Why get up and run the chance of going through the same embarrassing ritual again? Forget about it. You forgot about it before; you can forget about it again. If you're genuinely concerned about it, put it on your list of things to do ten years from now.

Just be the best *you* that you can be today. Do the same thing tomorrow. Keep doing that, and I guarantee that ten years from now, you'll be a person worth knowing, with or without a list.

Though I abhor lists, I do believe in having things in order. Everyone, old and young, should be organized. As I mentioned earlier, my mom taught that there should be a place for everything and everything should be in its place. It's a good philosophy to live by. The only difference between Mom and me was that I never know where those places were.

My family has been after me to tell them where important family documents are stored. I have kept complete and accurate records of every document of any significance relating to our family. I've kept them long; I've kept them well. But I have no idea where they are.

We planned a family meeting followed by a family dinner to discuss this supposed problem. However, I would have nixed the entire event had I known that it would degenerate into a ridiculing-Dad festival.

For many years, I've worked at home without the benefit of a secretary, an assistant, or an associate. I've devised my own filing system, which is quite innovative and astoundingly efficient . . . unless you want to find something. Then it becomes problematic.

I've refined the system over the years, making it more and more complex and elaborate. When I first started doing my own filing, I had only two drawers. One was marked "M" for "Miscellaneous." The other was marked "N" for "Nonmiscellaneous."

After a while, I was forced to add another drawer marked "L" for

"Lost." Eventually, this refinement made the other two drawers obsolete. Of course, I've made other adjustments over the years. Eventually, I developed my own unique system that is quite comprehensive. I added, changed, finagled, and created the present system—the one that the children were eager to learn about.

As I mentioned, all the important documents are contained within this system. I have them . . . somewhere. It became so all-inclusive, in fact, that when we moved a few years ago, my wife insisted that I clean out the overloaded filing cabinets. She thought it would be silly to spend good money to have moving men move useless paper. I agreed. I relentlessly discarded out-of-date documents.

But, wisely, I did make copies of all of them first.

Now to the family meeting where I was made sport of.

I patiently explained the finer points of my record-keeping to my offspring. Rather than being impressed, they giggled. Well, one daughter appreciated my efforts and complimented me. She said, "Dad, this is incredible. You should write a book explaining your system to the world."

Flattered, I said, "Really?"

She said, "Yes, you could call it *Office Filing—From A to G*."

They all chuckled again.

My son said, "If Dad ever wrote a dictionary, the words would be listed in chronological order."

They laughed again—more heartily.

Another daughter wanted to know why my life insurance policies were filed under "H."

"For 'Hope,'" I said. "I hope I don't need them for a long, long time."

She said, "This may sound dumb, but why didn't you just file them under 'I'?"

Now it was my turn to laugh, because I had her on this one. "I have them subfiled under 'I' also."

She asked, "For 'Insurance'?"

I said, "No. 'I' for 'in case *I* [I emphasized that word because my children seemed a little slow today] do need them before too long.'"

One daughter wanted to know how to find information on my various medications.

I said, "They're filed under 'P.'"

She said, "For 'Prescriptions,' right?"

I said, "No, for 'Pills.' I have a folder marked capital 'P' and another one marked lowercase 'p.'"

My son said, "And that's for . . .?"

It seemed obvious, but I explained anyway. "The capital 'P' is for big pills. The small 'p' is for little pills."

One daughter quipped, "It's a good thing you don't have any ointments."

I said, "I do. That's filed under 'S.'"

They all said, "For . . . ?"

I said, "For 'Stuff you rub on.'"

Now the giggling and chuckling surged into raucous laughter.

I said, "My system works fine for me. I can find anything I want at any time. And if I can't find something, I just convince myself that I didn't really want to find it in the first place."

One child said, "But, Dad, that doesn't do anyone else any good."

I told her, "I created this system for a personal reason."

"What personal reason?"

I said, "It's a secret."

They all said, "But, Dad, if anything happens to you, we'll never be able to find anything."

I said, "Oh, great. Now it's not a secret anymore."

Since my family didn't appreciate my filing system, I've since abandoned it. And do you know what? It's now easier for me to find things.

CHAPTER FIVE

YOUR TRUE SELF VERSUS YOUR FALSE SELF

"Know yourself. Don't accept your dog's admiration as conclusive evidence that you are wonderful." —Ann Landers

S elf-help is a forgiving philosophy. In fact, should you make a mistake, self-help will create for you a fall guy, a scapegoat, someone who will take the rap. You weren't wrong. You didn't commit the blunder. Your "false self" did.

What a blessing this is. It's like when you were a kid and had a little brother to blame. "Mom, I didn't do it. Freddie did it." You're off the hook, and Freddie's stuck in his room without dinner.

It's beautiful to have a partner in crime. It's loaded with benefits. Suppose you're riding on a crowded bus, a frail old woman gets on, and all the seats are occupied. Your true self would surely be gallant and offer this woman your seat. But you don't make that chivalrous gesture. No, you remain comfortably seated because your false self wants to keep the seat. The other riders may frown on your selfishness. You, too, may frown on your inconsiderate action. But it's not you doing this. It's your false self. So you ride forward guilt-free, and, as you travel on, you're still sitting comfortably. You get the best of both worlds. You soothe over your guilt because it's not really you who is guilty—it's your false self. And you get to keep your seat while this feeble woman struggles to keep her balance throughout the bumpy bus ride.

Nice, huh?

It's convenient to divide yourself into two separate people. One does whatever he or she wants; the other absorbs the condemnation. A comedian years ago kidded about this phenomenon. He claimed he went to see his therapist and the therapist advised, "We have to find the real you." And the comic said, "How come if there's another 'me' out there somewhere, you send this 'me' all the bills?" The comic added, "I'll tell you what: I'll pay you half. When you find the real me, he can pay you the rest of the money."

This can get to be a problem for those of us who have a few years behind us. I have trouble sometimes knowing where I am. I have neither the time nor the mental capacity to remember where the other "me"s are. If I go for a walk, I have to concentrate to get back to the same house I started from. I don't have time to round up all the other "me"s that may have wandered off in the meantime. I'm just a normal human being; I'm not a shepherd.

So this creating of another "me" can get confusing. A host of self-help authors maintain that what you think determines who you are. We've all heard variations of this reasoning before, and it seems to make sense. Your thoughts determine your actions. Your actions determine your fate. Consequently, what you think determines who you are. Simple enough.

However, later in the same breath, these authors declare that who you are determines how you think. It's rather like the chicken-and-egg dilemma. Which came first? Self-helpers suggest that you can change who you are by changing how you think but that you can't change how you think because you can only think according to who you are. Try figuring that one out.

It reminds me of an incident when I was a youngster. My mother took me into the central part of the city to do some shopping with her. Unfortunately, I was my false self at the time and was misbehaving. My mom got so frustrated with me that she shouted, "The next time I take you out, I'm leaving you home."

I was so distracted trying to figure out what she said that I didn't have time to behave badly from that point on.

It's apparent, though, that dividing ourselves into separate parts can be confusing. Take, for example, this one day when I was feeling particularly sorry for myself. Then an idea popped into my head that no matter how bad off I was feeling, there was always somebody on our planet who was worse off than I was. It was an attempt to cheer myself up, but then I began to think that this concept was dumb.

Suppose someone has a painful toothache. Surely somewhere, someone has a toothache and an earache at the same time. They're worse off than the first person, right? But somewhere else, someone has a toothache, an earache, and a painful sensation running from his buttocks down to his left knee. This poor guy is worse off than the first two.

What sort of cheerful consolation is this supposed to provide? If you're depressed, you shouldn't suddenly be cheered up just because you know someone is more depressed than you are. If anything, that should depress you even more than your depressed friend. So now maybe you're worse off than the guy with the toothache, earache, and pain shooting from his backside to his knee. Dumb.

Besides, it's false logic. There are 7.2 billion people on Earth presently. Somebody has to be worse off than all the others. Some poor clown is sitting somewhere knowing that 7,199,999,999 people are doing better than he is.

Well, on this particular day, I felt like that person. I felt like the most victimized, put upon, demoralized, unfortunate, despondent, dismal soul on earth. So there. I hoped that cheered up the other 7,199,999,999 others.

Happy to be of service.

And then I heard:

That's probably the stupidest thing I ever heard.

"Who said that?"

Me.

"Who are you?"

Me? I'm you.

"You're me?"

That's right, I'm you.

"So I'm talking to myself."

Well, we're not really talking; *we're communicating with thoughts, but, in a sense, yes, you're talking to yourself.*

"Great. So now, along with all my other problems, I'm going insane."

You're not crazy. Everybody talks to themselves.

"Well, I don't remember talking to myself before."

That's because for the most part, you've always ignored me. Remember when you were going to buy that new Ford and I said to you, "Hey, why don't you consider a Chevy? The new Malibu is pretty nice."

"I don't remember that."

Like I said, you usually ignored me.

"Who are you, really?"

I'm your better self.

"Wait a minute. Who decided that? How come you're automatically better than me?"

You just said that out of 7.2 billion people, you were number 7,199,999,999. How could I be any worse?

"So I take it you're smarter than me?"

Yes. Oh, gracious, yes. Absolutely, yes. No doubt in the world about it, yes. There's positively no question—

"OK, OK . . . I get the idea. Are you one of those mystics who sees all things and knows all things?"

You can lay off the sarcasm. No, I don't know all things. I just know more about what's right for you than you do.

"Let me get things straight here for a minute. Let me review quickly. You're me, right?"

Right.

"And I'm you, right?"

Right.

"So we're the same person. How can I be having two different thoughts and actually arguing with myself when there's only one of me here?"

Everybody has different thoughts. Remember when you were in school, they used to tell you that you had a good angel sitting on your right shoulder telling you to do what's right. But on your left shoulder was the bad angel— the devil with horns and a pitchfork and a long tail. He was telling you to do what's evil. You were arguing with yourself back then.

"Yeah, but that was just a cartoon. It was just a way of picturing what was going on in my head."

Exactly. It was going on in your head. It was a cute little cartoon, but it's basically real. You do talk to yourself. Remember when you went on that trip to Rome and you stood in the Sistine Chapel looking up at the Michelangelo painting on the ceiling?

"Yeah, so what?"

So, you said to yourself, Wow, I'm actually here in the Sistine Chapel looking up at the Michelangelo painting on the ceiling. *Who do you think was saying that to you? It was another part of you who couldn't believe that you were actually standing in the Sistine Chapel looking up at the Michelangelo painting on the ceiling.*

"You're reaching a little bit now, aren't you?"

Not really. Why would you have to tell yourself you were there? You knew you were there; you didn't have to tell yourself that. It just shows that whatever you do, there's a part of you observing what you do and analyzing what you do. And that other part of you talks to you, and that's what you're doing now.

"That's what *we're* doing now."

No, that's what you're *doing now. There's only one of you. I'm just a different part of you.*

"The smarter part."

Yes. Oh, gracious, yes. Absolutely, yes. No doubt in the world about it, yes. There's positively no question—

"OK . . . you can knock that off anytime you want. Let me ask you this, though. If you're me and you've done all the same things I've done, been all the same places, had all the same experiences, know the same friends, and everything else, how come you think you know more about what's right for me than I do?"

That's easy. Because you've been listening to too many people who aren't you. They tell you things that are right for them but not necessarily right for you. Bottom line: they don't care about you; they care about themselves.

"Which people?"

Everybody who's not you. Friends, advisors, people to whom your business is none of their business, your parents, your relatives.

"Hold on. You're saying none of these people care about me. Mom and Dad—you remember them—they didn't care about me?"

Sure, they cared about you, but they cared about you from their perspective, not from your point of view. Not all of these people mean any harm, but they just don't know you as well as you know you. They know what they want for you but not what you might want for yourself.

"You're telling me, then, that anytime people offer me advice, I should reject it because it's what they want and not what I want."

You should decide what's right for you. Suppose you went to a restaurant—a very nice restaurant—but when they handed out the menus, they didn't give them to you but to the people at the table next to you. Then they told those people, "You order the meal for him." You wouldn't want to go back there anymore. Now the waiter may recommend something, or the people at the next table may tell you they had the Veal Parmigiana and it was delicious, but you should decide for yourself what you want to eat.

"Isn't it just possible that maybe a parent or a friend or a trusted advisor could just by sheer coincidence be telling me what's right for me?"

It's absolutely possible. But how will you know?

"That's a good question. Since you're the smarter of us two—"

The smarter of us one.

"Very clever. Since you're smarter, you tell me—how will I know?"

You'll know because you'll know.

"Oh, that's good. For someone who claims to be so smart, you make some pretty dumb statements."

It's not as dumb as you might think. As I said earlier, you have been listening for too long to people who are not you. Many of them have different things that they feel are perfect for you and for many different reasons. By coincidence, some suggestions may be right for you; several are not. But you've been hearing them for so long that they've confused you. Nevertheless, inside, you have a feeling for what you truly desire—for something that you love. That is what's right for you.

"Again, though: How do I know?"

You base your decision on love, not fear.

"What?"

You have to decide what you truly, really desire. You can't base that on what your friends think, what your relatives say, what tradition and common sense dictate, what's going to make you a lot of money—

"Wait a minute. Hold it."

The mention of money got your attention, huh?

"Yeah, it did. What if making a lot of money is what I really love? What if making a lot of money is what I really want to do?"

Then go for it.

"But you just said that making a decision based on making a lot of money wasn't what I should do."

No. I said making a decision based purely on making a lot of money wouldn't be right for you if it wasn't what you wanted to do. There's nothing wrong with wanting to make a lot of money. Many people have that goal, and they're perfectly content pursuing it. BUT—and it's a big BUT—deciding to go after a lot of money instead of doing what you truly want to do is listening to those others again.

"But what you're advocating is total recklessness."

How?

"I need money."

Do you need a lot of money?

"I need enough."

How much is enough?

"Well, I don't want to go traipsing after some highfalutin goal and wind up with no place to live and nothing to eat."

So now we're back to making a decision based on fear. You're afraid of going broke.

"Well, yeah, I am. What's wrong with that?"

The only thing wrong with it is to use it as a basis for making a decision. Start with what you desire, not what you're afraid of.

"But what good is pursuing a dream if you wind up broke?"

See, you're listening to those others *again. They're telling you that if you do what you truly want to do, you'll wind up a pauper. Have you ever heard of Phyllis Diller?*

"Certainly I have. Everybody has. She was a legendary comedian."

She wasn't always a legendary comedian. For a long time, she was a housewife struggling to raise a family and make ends meet.

"Yeah, so?"

So, she tells us in her autobiography that one day, she picked up a book called The Magic of Believing *by Claude Bristol. It inspired her to go for her dreams. She read the book, studied it, applied its principles, and began to chase her dream of becoming a comedian.*

"Oh, sure, I get it. And the rest is history? Right?"

Not exactly. She struggled at first, but she persevered. Whatever the details were, it worked.

"Well, good for her."

Yes, it was good for her, and I don't know if you noticed it or not, but she didn't go broke. It's possible to go after what you want and not starve to death. It's possible to pursue a dream and make a comfortable living. It's even conceivable that a person could seek out a goal and make a fortune doing it.

"It's rare, though."

That's the fear speaking again. That's listening to those others again instead of me—instead of yourself. When we first started this discussion, you were number 7.2 billion out of 7.2 billion people.

"That was pure hyperbole."

I know it was, but it still showed that you were feeling pretty low about yourself. You wanted better. All I'm saying is that the first step in moving you up the ladder is to honestly, sincerely, and realistically focus on what is right for you. Don't worry about what others think or don't think. And make your decision based on genuine desire. Keep the element of fear out of it. That's the absolute first step. Then you can build from there.

Having two separate selves can get confusing. And now it can get even more involved. If you're going to have arguments and discussions between your true self and your false self, someone has to be the arbiter. Someone has to decide who wins the arguments. Remember how one of the selves mentions that it's like having a good angel on one shoulder and a bad angel on the other shoulder? That means there must be someone in the middle providing the shoulders. Now we've got three people involved. It's getting crowded.

We older folks don't like crowds. So maybe we should forget the true-self-and-false-self theory and just stay with who we are.

CHAPTER SIX

POSITIVE THINKING

"A positive attitude may not solve all your problems, but it
will annoy enough people to make it worth the effort."
—Herm Albright

onsider the tale of a common, ordinary working man, whom
we'll call Charlie. Like all of us, Charlie wanted to get ahead.
He was positive about it. He knew that he would enjoy success
eventually. Not much seemed to be working for him to date, but he remained confident, positive. It would happen.

Charlie was always fond of hats and wore them well. He wore them
with a jaunty, Sinatra-like tilt to them. He looked good, and he felt good
wearing them. Somehow Charlie was sure that hats would be involved in
his future. He might design them, manufacture them, or perhaps make his
fortune selling them. Whichever avenue he rode to fulfillment, hats, he
knew, would be a major factor.

Then Charlie had a sort of epiphany. Each night he would dream of
hats. Hats, of course, were always on his mind, but these recurring dreams
were a new experience.

Charlie took those dreams as an omen. He was positive they would change his life, but how?

Then it hit him. He'd take all the money he had saved to this point and invest it wisely . . . at the racetrack.

At the track, though, Charlie couldn't find a thoroughbred in any of the races with "hat" in its name. The closest he could come was one horse named "Fancy Lid." *Close enough*, Charlie thought, and he put his savings on this dapple gray to win.

Charlie stood at the rail and cheered the animal on. Fancy Lid was doing well when they came to the final turn. He strode valiantly, threatening all the way. However, Fancy Lid didn't cross the finish line first. Charlie was wiped out. Some horse with the dopey name of "Sombrero" beat him.

Charlie put everything he had into positive thinking when perhaps the purchase of a Spanish–English dictionary might have served him better.

Thinking positively is an admirable trait that produces many worthwhile benefits. To begin, it helps us begin. Overcoming the inertia of any project is a challenge. One of the reasons why we procrastinate is because we fear we won't complete the task satisfactorily. "Why should I start writing a book," people say to themselves, "when I know I'll never finish it, and if I do, no one will read it, and if they do, no one will like it?" No book would ever get written that was approached with that mindset. But with a brilliant idea and a positive feeling about its appeal, you'll turn on the computer and start churning out pages.

There was a teacher once who assigned a rather complicated mathematical puzzle to his class. To half of the room, he simply stated the problem. To the other half of the room, he told the students secretively that there was no solution to this particular problem. There actually was a valid solution, but he purposely misled the second half to prove a point.

At the end of the session, the first half had all yielded results. Some of them were wrong, but they came up with an attempt at a solution. The second half of the room had no results. They didn't bother trying to solve the problem since they felt that there was no correct answer. They were misled by a negative outlook and it kept them from even trying. A positive attitude encourages at least the attempt.

A positive outlook generates enthusiasm for our task, whatever it might be. Knowing we're going to be successful prompts us to do whatever must be done to ensure that success. We do the preparatory work joyfully. We follow each step of the process passionately. We apply the finishing touches with pride. We're eager to progress because we know we'll be pleased with the results.

A positive feeling promotes confidence. You often read in sports news that a specific player or a given team was "in the zone." That indicates they were performing above average—they could seemingly do no wrong. Playing with confidence can produce such results. And who doesn't want to be better than he or she normally is? Who doesn't want to play a little better than he or she is capable of?

A positive outlook reduces stress. The pressure of trying to perform well can inhibit our execution. Golfers experience this phenomenon often. One player was faced with a difficult shot that had to carry a long way over water. He stepped up to the ball, stood over it for a moment, began his swing, and whacked the ball solidly. It sailed over the water and landed comfortably and safely on the grass on the other side. A playing partner said to him, "That was a great shot over the water." The golfer replied, "What water?"

In that golfer's mind, the water didn't exist. Consequently, he hit the shot without pressure and without fear. His positive attitude yielded a fantastic golf shot. That sort of thinking applies in other circumstances, too.

Positive thinking can make any task more enjoyable. No one enjoys losing or failing. No one enjoys predicting that they will lose or fail. We have more exuberance when we know we will do great—or we at least give ourselves a reasonable shot at success. In fact, some self-helpers proclaim that simply feeling that you're going to lose will become a self-fulfilling prophecy. In other words, if you think you're going to lose, you're going to lose. One quote went so far as to state, "Whether you think you're going to win or you think you're going to lose, you're right."

With confidence and a positive outlook, you are perceived as a winner. That's a big plus on going on to become an eventual winner. Jimmy Connor at his peak was a formidable opponent in tennis. Once he got a lead, his challenger would be tempted to concede. The challenger would feel he had no chance of overcoming the deficit. However, often, the opponent would get the lead. But he would worry so much about losing that edge that he eventually would lose that advantage. In other words, being perceived as a winner gave Jimmy Connor added leverage to become the winner.

To be fair, though, there is also a definite downside to positive thinking: it implies a certain amount of negative thinking. In fact, positive thinking might also be called "nonnegative thinking." In order to be successful, you're forced to consider the potential failures. There is a philosophical axiom that states, "In the absence of what is not, what is, is not." In order for something to be, there must be something that it is not. For instance, night is required to have day. If there were no night, there would be no need for the term "day." Day, in essence, is really "non-night." Confusing, huh?

Let's try this. Suppose that all people were exactly the same height. Let's arbitrarily pick six feet even. If we accept that premise, then we must accept that there are no short people and no tall people. There are only people of the same six-foot height.

So positive thinking requires some thought to the negative. Here's an example:

In the days of live television, an actor was hired to play a role in an hour-long drama. This actor had only one line. He was cast as the foreman of the jury, and his line was "Guilty."

Keep in mind the show was live, not on tape or on film. They could do no retakes or inserts. It was what it was. When the time came for this actor to deliver his line, he said, "Not guilty."

All the other performers and the director were flabbergasted. The actor blew his line and changed the entire direction of the show. Mercifully, some of the experienced actors managed to cover his mistake and return the show to its intended direction.

This happened because the actor, trying to be positive, introduced the necessary negative. While he was backstage preparing to go on, he kept thinking of the negative and saying to himself, "Don't say 'Not guilty' . . . don't say 'Not guilty' . . ." It was so embedded in his mind that when the cue was delivered, he said, "Not guilty."

The basic idea behind positive thinking is you become what you think you are. If you think you are rich, you'll be rich. If you think you're powerful, you'll someday be powerful. If you think you're talented, you'll be talented. If you think this works, you're young and gullible. Those of us who are more mature are somewhat skeptical. When we go to a boxing match, we don't always think the boxer who thinks he's going to win is going to win. We're more inclined to think the boxer who hits fastest, hardest, and most frequently will win.

There was an entertainer who told his audience, "That's the end of my act, but I'm going to do my encore number right now. Many performers will leave the stage and wait a moment while the appreciative applause of the audience brings them back on stage for one or two encore numbers. I'm not going to do that. I've been burned too many times."

That's how we old-timers feel—we've been burned too many times. We admire the positive attitude and admit that it has many benefits. At the same time, we realize that it's not a magic bullet that works without fail.

The following is a confession of one of my positive-thinking experiments that sort of backfired:

My wife had been expecting a package. When it was delivered and she opened it, she was quite upset.

"What's wrong?" I asked.

"I ordered these shirts for the boys ["the boys" is our code name for our grandsons], and they sent the wrong items, the wrong colors, and the wrong sizes. I ordered medium, and they sent extra large."

I said, "Other than that, were they all right?"

My wife wasn't in the mood for attempted humor. She said, "I'm very upset by this."

I looked at the merchandise and the documents and said, "I'll handle this."

Notice I didn't say, "I'll look into this." I didn't say, "I'll see what I can do." I didn't say, "I'll try to get this fixed." Those statements are all vague and without promised results. No, I was positive in my approach. I said boldly and confidently, "I'll handle this."

And so I set out to handle it.

I called the company, and after one or two rings, I heard a robotic voice say, "Your call is very important to us. Please stay on the line. The expected wait time is approximately five minutes." Then there was a click, and they began playing atrocious music that would make a five-minute wait seem like a two-hour-and-twenty-seven-minute wait. This is the kind of music they played to expedite Noriega's surrender. I endured it for slightly over a minute, then hung up and redialed.

After two or three rings, I heard, "Your call is very important to us. Please stay on the line. The expected wait time is approximately—" Then I got lucky. I heard a click and another robotic voice said, "Thank you for calling Almond Clothing. If you're calling to place an order, press 1. If you're calling to cancel an order, press 2." I wasn't calling for either one of those situations, so I hesitated.

Hesitating is a mistake when you're dealing with a robot. I heard a click followed by a dial tone. Almond Clothing's automated voice hung up on me.

I dialed again, still positive—but I do admit I pushed each button a little bit harder this time. It was my illogical way of expressing my displeasure with the rather rude digital voice. Predictably, a robot thanked me again and told me how important my call was to them. It then asked me to press either 1 or 2.

I tried to outsmart their automatons by pushing 1. I thought that if they thought I was going to buy something, they might be more accommodating. I was right. I heard a few clicks and a much more pleasant

robot answered: "Thank you for calling Almond Clothing. It's our pleasure to serve you. Please press the catalog number of the item you wish
to order." They called my bluff.

I didn't want to order anything from their catalog, so I was stymied. I
hesitated. As we've already learned, hesitating is a mistake when dealing
with a robot. This time, even the more pleasant artificial voice hung up
on me.

I dialed again, pressing the numbers even harder this time. I got the
same preamble, but this time I pressed 2. The last time, 1 didn't work, so
I had no other alternative but to press 2, which was the button for cancel-
ling an order. The voice again thanked me for calling Almond Clothing
but with stern, challenging overtones. It said, not pleasantly, "Please
press the catalog number of the item you wish to cancel." Once again, I
was at a robotically generated dead end. I didn't have a catalog number
for the item I wanted to return, because I didn't want to return an item.

But this time, I cleverly outsmarted the system. Before they could dis-
connect, I pressed 0, thinking that would get me a live operator. It got me
another counterfeit voice that said, "That is not a valid response." Click . . .
dial tone.

It appeared I was out of options, but I couldn't allow that. I had
promised my wife: "I will handle it." Therefore, handle it I must. I looked
the company up on the Internet and found a phone number for the corporate headquarters.

Again, remaining positive, I dialed that number. I heard, "Thank you
for calling Almond Clothing. May I help you?"

It was a live person. I was astounded. Who would have thought that
Almond Clothing would hire actual living, breathing people? Of course,
I guess that made sense. Someone must have picked out the wrong shirts
in the wrong colors and the wrong sizes and sent them to our house.

I must have stayed amazed too long because the live person repeated,
"May I help you?"

I quickly said, "Yes." I knew my call was very important to them, so I
didn't want them to hang up on me again.

I said, "I have a problem with an order I placed."

She said, "Oh, I apologize, because your orders are very important to us."

I quickly yelled, "Don't hang up."

She said, "Oh, no, sir. We at Almond Clothing don't hang up on our loyal customers."

I felt like saying that they should tell that to their robots, but I was determined to remain positive, so I said nothing sarcastic.

She said, "What items did you order?

I said, "Three men's shirts."

She said, "Oh, all right, I'll transfer you to the men's clothing customer service department. But before I do, thank you for calling Almond Clothing. Your calls are very important to us."

"Thank you," I said.

Then I heard click . . . dial tone.

For a company that seemed to relish my calls so much, they sure could dismiss them quickly.

I redialed the corporate offices of Almond Clothing. I heard the phone ring three times and then I heard an animated voice say, "Thank you for calling Almond Clothing. Your call is very important to us. Unfortunately, due to an extraordinary amount of calls, we have to put you on hold."

I thought, *The amount of calls is extraordinary because they must be all the people calling back after you and your robots hung up on them.*

The fake voice went on, "Please stay on the line. The expected wait time is approximately ten minutes."

When the horrific music began playing, I hung up . . . decisively, almost vehemently.

My wife said, "Did you handle it?"

I said, "I've got the solution to the problem."

My wife said, "OK. What should I do with the extra-large shirts?"

I thought positively. I said, "Tell our grandsons to put on some weight."

CHAPTER SEVEN

VISUALIZATION

"I visualize a time when we will be to robots what dogs are to humans, and I'm rooting for the machines." —Claude Shannon

There's a teacher at a California college who has amassed an amazing record. His students have sold well over one million dollars' worth of articles to various magazines, both regional and national. These were not former students who went on to sell their product after they had completed his course. No—these articles were sold while the youngsters were in his class. The total, of course, was cumulative, but all of the pieces were written, accepted, and paid for while the students were enrolled.

One million dollars in writing fees is an impressive total. Many free-lancers would enjoy earning that in a lifetime. This teacher's students did it during the short time they were studying how to write. The instructor not only concentrated on teaching them to construct a solid magazine article but also coached them on selling what they wrote. That can be an important factor in a career.

The teacher was justifiably proud of his achievement. In fact, he created a testament to the class's marketing success. He decorated the interior of his classroom with the acceptance letters and reproductions of the checks that accompanied them. It snaked around the room like a giant tapeworm that kept growing and growing and growing.

The students were rightly pleased with their accomplishments, too. Each new student wanted to become a part of this "Chain of Fame." Past students had done well; this class can do equally as well. If they could do it, we can do it.

And so the chain continued to grow. It eventually outgrew the classroom and spilled over into the college corridors. Other instructors objected to the blatant self-promotion because it highlighted not only the one teacher's accomplishments with his students but also the other instructors' own lack of sales success. However, the college authorities allowed it to continue. It was valuable PR that attracted aspiring writers to their curriculum. It was an inspiration to young writers. It was a learning tool, and it was practical. Pupils wanted to study under this professor because they not only fulfilled their curriculum requirements but also had a shot at making a bit of extra cash.

The total sales figures may have grown even more since I first became aware of it. The Chain of Fame may have flowed out from the corridors onto the steps leading up to the college's main building. It might even wind along the tree-lined driveway that leads onto the campus. Heck, it might even replace the white lines that run along the interstate highways that lead to the school. So long as this enterprising teacher inspires his class and these eager students keep selling, the chain will expand.

What did this teacher do that generated so much enthusiasm and success? He reduces it to two simple words: query letters. For one month during his writing course, the students are required to come up with a salable idea every single day. It must be a different idea each day. Not only do they have to create the idea, but they must write a query letter explaining it and submit that letter to a suitable periodical. This demand is not negotiable; it's required to pass the course.

This means that each student is forced to write and submit query letters for at least thirty articles during that month. Compare that to the average number of articles submitted by college students each year to paying publications. That average number is . . . roughly . . . oh, about . . . none. So if you take that average number and multiply by, let's say, $300 per article, the amount of money received is . . . roughly . . . oh, about . . . nothing.

But the math for this class is astounding. Let's say this teacher has thirty students. During the critical month, those students would be submitting 900 separate article ideas for publication. For our hypothetical calculations, suppose only 1.5 percent of those sell. That works out to 13.5 articles sold that month. Multiply that number by $300 per article, and you wind up with a whopping $4,050 total. That's a commendable record for a group of youngsters who would just as soon show up in class and say, "The dog ate my homework."

There are several factors contributing to the extraordinary success rate of these college kids. First, the instructor is trumping their natural inclination to procrastinate. These students most likely feel that there is plenty of time to submit query letters and sell articles later. Once they get to know what they're doing and have their career off to a promising start, then they can think creatively and pursue sales. This teacher doesn't allow that. "Do it now," he says. "Do it today," he demands.

He appeals to their competitive nature. He shows them what other classes have done and challenges them to outdo them. Collectively they say, "If you did it, we can do it." And so they do.

He offers his students hope. A feeling of hopelessness is natural to beginners. But now their teacher is proving to them that other beginners sold their work. It's possible that this class can also.

Also, the instructor is playing the percentages. Send out 900 query letters in one month, and you're bound to get a greater return than if you send out no query letters in one month. (We've already done the math.)

Self-helpers maintain that a Chain of Fame is a measurable factor in achievement also. They advocate that you should "see" your goal—visualize it. They recommend a concrete, graphic, visible representation of your goal. An abstract goal is insufficient for their purposes.

This instructor's Chain of Fame transformed an amorphous goal of selling a piece of writing into a solid image. The acceptance letters could be seen and read. The check was clearly printed and signed. These were not vague concepts any longer; they were now ink on paper.

Some volumes suggest keeping a scrapbook that illustrates your dreams and goals. Are you eager to have a new and beautiful home? Then paste photos of beautiful homes into your scrapbook and peruse it frequently. Ignore the fact that those homes are presently owned by someone else. Ignore the fact that many of them may be geographically undesirable. A dream home you are attracted to may be in Kennebunkport, Maine, while you make your living in Eugene, Oregon. That's OK . . . just don't paste images of the commute each morning.

The idea is that you are to look at these pictures so much that it forces a desire into your soul and, somehow or another, that desire combined with vivid visualization will provide whatever means you need to acquire a new and beautiful home.

Another recommended gimmick is to assemble a montage of your dreams. Paste photos of your goal onto a bulletin board that's prominently displayed so that you're constantly seeing the results of your quest. The image never lets you forget the dream that you're seeking.

Some say that if you want to lose weight, you should gather photographs of people with slim figures and put them on the mirror in your bathroom so it's the first thing you see in the morning and the last thing you see at night. This will help you visualize your future skinny self. Of course, if you're too much overweight, it might be unwise to spend too much time in front of a mirror—especially one that has the image of someone with a heavenly figure in view. The comparison may be traumatic.

I knew one gentleman who was so self-conscious about his girth that he refused even to look at the numbers on the scale when he stepped on to it. He purchased instead a "speaking scale." It would read out his weight instead of him having to look at the numbers. He abandoned that idea when he stepped onto the scale one day and it said, "Come back when you're alone."

There is probably validity to all these concepts, but again, they apply more to the younger readers and dreamers than to us older folk. Our eyesight begins to fail at a certain point. I may post pictures of my dream house all over the place. And that might be just the motivation to get off my bottom and work to get that dream house, but then I'll find when I do acquire it that it's blurry.

I, for one, am "visualization challenged." I have trouble picturing real things, so I'm definitely hampered in conjuring up images of vague concepts. This following tale should convince you:

My wife and I once enjoyed an excursion through a national park somewhere near Tucson, Arizona. It was a beautiful canyon with gorgeous natural foliage, waterfalls, swimming holes, picnic areas, hiking trails—all of Mother Nature's finest. We signed up for a tram ride of about three and a half miles up the mountain and, not surprisingly, three and a half miles back down. Our tour guide was a delightful park ranger, a cross between Smokey the Bear and Phyllis the Diller. The tour guide knew all of the flora and fauna, the history of the canyon, and every peak and crevice and had amusing and clever quips for the entire jaunt.

That's when I discovered how advanced my visualization impairment had become. I learned that I apparently can't see what others can.

During the tour, our guide said, "If you look towards the mountains on the right side of the tram . . ." and everyone immediately leaned that way and gawked.

The guide continued, ". . . you'll notice the outcropping there that looks like a bear's nose." With impeccable timing, she waited a beat or two, and then everyone on the tram said, "Ohhh . . . yeah," and pointed towards the bear's nose-like formation. Everyone but me.

"Isn't that amazing?" my wife said.

"What?" I said.

"The rock that looks like a bear's nose."

"I don't see any rock that looks like a bear's nose."

My wife asked, "Where are you looking?"

"Up."

"Up where?"

I said, "Up the bear's nose, I suppose, but I can't see any bear's nose."

"Forget about it," my wife said. "We're past it now anyway."

It didn't matter, because as soon as we got out of view of the alleged bear's nose, our guide pointed out another formation. "Off to the left of the tram," she said, "you'll notice what we call 'Bobcat Head Peak.' Does anyone know why?"

The entire tram shouted back, "Because it's shaped like a bobcat's head!" Everyone yelled that except me. I couldn't see it.

My wife asked, "Don't you see the two ears sticking up?"

"All I see are rocks."

"Well, of course you see rocks," she said. "But some of them are shaped like bobcat ears."

"No, they're not," I said probably a bit too loudly.

The entire tram, including the park ranger, screamed back, "Yes, they are!"

I was somewhat embarrassed and more than a little frightened. These sightseers were beginning to get hostile.

The tour guide said, "We're now approaching 'Skunk Crevice.'"

I figured if you can't beat 'em, join 'em, so I pointed to the mountain wall and proclaimed, "I see it! I do! I see where the rock is discolored and it looks just like the stripe on the back of a skunk."

The park ranger said, "It's off to the left of the tram."

(I had been pointing to the right of the tram.)

It made no difference. I didn't see anything on either side of the tram that looked anything like a skunk.

The others definitely saw it, because they all tried to get me to see it.

Someone said, "It's right above the rock that looks like a quail."

Another said, "Find the one that looks like angel wings and go down and to the right."

"It's right next to the beaver-shaped rock," someone else offered.

I couldn't see any of those.

Then someone said, "Open your eyes, you clown."

That last remark opened my eyes, metaphorically speaking. It convinced me that I should just stop looking. Let those who could see, see. Let them enjoy the critters that were hiding among the crooks and crevices in the cliffs. I'd just sit sullenly and think that if Mother Nature had wanted me to revel in those sights, she would have put signs on them, maybe with arrows pointing to the bear's nose or the bobcat's ears. I never looked right or left after that, no matter what instruction Phyllis the Diller shouted out.

When the tram stopped, I banged my head as I was disembarking.

"He can't even see the tram," someone whispered—not quietly enough.

"Are you all right?" my wife asked.

I told her I was.

"No, you're not," she said. "You have a nasty bruise there."

"Where?" I said.

She said, "Right on your forehead." She took a closer look. Others from our tram gathered around and looked, too.

One said, "Yeah, that's a nasty bruise. It looks a little bit like a jackrabbit."

The others all pointed at my forehead and said, "Ooooh . . . yeah. . . ."

I've been antivisualization ever since.

CHAPTER EIGHT

MEDITATION

"You should sit in meditation for twenty minutes a day—unless you're too busy; then you should sit for an hour."
—Old Zen saying

Meditation is the fuel that drives the self-help vehicle. There are other facets to self-improvement, but according to most of the experts, meditation in some form is essential. Your family car has many parts, too—engine block, pistons, valves, drive shaft, carburetor, and many others. They're all essential—well, you pay for them whether they're essential or not. But none of them will work if the arrow on the fuel indicator is on "E." You need gas to get the car going.

That's what they tell us about meditation. There are probably more important facets of self-help, but they don't work, so they tell us, without meditation. Usually, daily meditation is recommended—sometimes two or three sessions a day.

All of the promoters of achievement tout contemplation. It's the *sine qua non* of the advancement theories. "If you don't meditate, forget about being great."

There are many different brands of fuel that you can use. Your car engine will run regardless of which gas station you fill up at. Similarly, there are various styles of meditation. Mercifully, they leave the choice to you.

Right off the bat, though, we older citizens can discard yoga. With yoga, you manipulate your body into strangely grotesque (or beautiful, depending on your point of view) positions. There are hundreds of them, and they all have intriguing names. There's the "awkward chair" pose that either looks like an awkward chair or someone who is sitting in an awkward chair. Or it could resemble someone who has been sitting in an awkward chair and is now suffering the consequences. There's the "cat-cow" stretch, which probably looks like a cat stretching or a cow stretching, depending on your particular body shape. There's one called the "cat face" pose. I have no idea what that resembles, but apparently the cow said, "I want no part of this one." There's a "down dog" pose. Use your imagination for this one. And an "elephant trunk" pose and a "down dog" split. Just reading the word "split" should frighten you away from that one.

In yoga, you force your body into any of these suggested poses or positions. Then you hold that pose and contemplate. Your mind is free of stress and complaints. It's totally absorbed in wondering how you ever got your body into this position. More important, it's captivated by the idea of how you're ever going to get your body out of this position.

If you ever catch me in a yoga position, it means I've fallen down a flight of stairs and that's how I landed.

There is a meditation formula in which you think of absolutely nothing. For most of us, it's comparable to our college experience. The idea is to keep your mind absolutely blank. If an idea should pop into your head, you should banish it immediately. But then, as soon as you think you got rid of the intruding thought, aren't you thinking again? If you have a head full of nothing, obviously, you can't have a head full of negative thoughts or distracting thoughts. That seems like a good thing. But it was Descartes, dubbed "the father of modern philosophy," who said, "I think, therefore I am." So if you stop thinking, don't you run the risk of disappearing? It hardly seems like an intelligent gamble.

To confuse things even more, there's also a meditation that recommends that you try to think of everything. You gaze at a rose, and you see all parts of that beautiful, delicate flower. You breathe as the rose would breathe. You feel as the rose would feel. You welcome the sunshine on your petals. You invite the bee to partake of your nectar. You *become* the rose. Is that good? Well, parts of it are, probably, but it has its downside, too. First of all, all your suits are going to need altering. Try getting on a crowded streetcar with all those thorns you've acquired, and surely a fight is going to break out.

There's a meditation in which you concentrate on your breathing. All you have to do is sit and breathe but think about each breath you take. Follow the precious air you inhale as it goes into your mouth, over your tongue, over your uvula. Stay with it as it goes down your throat and into your lungs. Feel it swell your lungs. Feel it give new life to the worn-out blood that rushes to the lungs to be refreshed.

Be honest, now. Doesn't this feel a tad voyeuristic to you? Isn't your own breath entitled to a modicum of privacy? The poor particles of air go inside your body trying to get away from the hubbub of the outside world. It probably entered your body with the thought of a brief bit of rest and relaxation, and here you are becoming a mental Peeping Tom. It's a bit sick and probably should be illegal.

There's a meditation practice in which you concentrate on the present moment. The problem here is that there is no present moment. Once the "present" arrives, it immediately becomes "the past." If you concentrate on it, you're focusing on the past, which is verboten in this procedure. Now, maybe you think you can get a jump on it. Think about the present moment before it arrives. That way, you might be able to capture it before it dissolves into the past. You're probably not quick enough to do that, but even if you were, you would be thinking about the future. If the moment hasn't arrived yet, it can't be the present. And it hasn't slipped by yet, so it can't be the past. So if it's neither the present nor the past, what is it? It's the future and, again, it's verboten to think of the future with this process. You can only think of the present, which immediately becomes the past.

Maybe a good meditation device would be to sit in a comfortable chair, close your eyes, and try to contemplate what this paragraph was about.

There's a type of meditation where you sit quietly and comfortably and simply repeat a given phrase over and over again. The phrase is called a "mantra." One of the most popular is the one syllable "aum."

Some of us older folks may be practicing this procedure unwittingly. Many of us make a noise that resembles "aum" each time we get up out of a chair. It may not qualify as meditation, because we don't have to think about it. It just pops out. We move to get up and something inside of us says, "I believe saying 'aum' will help in standing up." So we go "aum." Often, we embellish it so that it becomes "aumph."

My wife often says, "Do you have to make that silly noise each time you get up out of a chair?"

I say, "You mean that 'aum' sound?"

She says, "No, I mean the creaking and the crunching as you stand."

(That's a whole other thing that has nothing to do with meditation or its benefits.)

Some manuals suggest that it's advisable to meditate to soothing, re- laxing music. Our generation realizes, though, that ever since Perry Como left the scene, there is no such thing as soothing, relaxing music.

Along those same lines, much advice on meditating promotes it as a great relaxer, a stress-reliever, a quieting of the mind. But they also warn that meditating and focusing on whatever they want you to focus on can be hard work and difficult to learn. They caution you that the process can be frustrating. It almost seems as though you're in pretty good shape with a day that is treating you fairly. Not much is bothering you. It seems a perfect time to improve your life with meditation. So you assume a com- fortable position, relax your mind and body, and then you have trouble doing whatever they've advised you to do. So you get frustrated. They've warned that you'll get frustrated. You might even get angry. So now you're all stressed out because you're having trouble relieving stress. It's kind of like those people who enjoy playing golf because it's so relaxing and then throw their clubs in the lake.

I once attended a lecture on "relaxation." There were about 1,500 people in the theatre, and the lecturer would lead us in a meditation that would soothe our souls and relax our bodies. The result would be enhanced performance and more intense focus. It was thrilling to be a part of it. The speaker was excellent. He had a calming, soothing voice. He spoke in a hypnotizing monotone. Just listening to him was calming yet exhilarating.

He advised us to assume a comfortable position. That was relatively easy because the theatre seats were well padded and slid back and forth so that no matter how you arranged your body in those chairs, it was comfortable.

He instructed us that they would dim the lights in the theatre and that we should close our eyes. At first, this seemed like overkill. Why dim the lights if we're going to close our eyes? That's like wearing a belt and suspenders to hold your pants up. One or the other is not carrying its weight. However, this was his lecture, so I went along with it. As the lights went down, I closed my eyes obediently.

Now that tranquilizing voice told us to travel to our favorite retreat. We were to envision ourselves in a place that was beautiful and peaceful. I put myself in a rowboat in the middle of a large lake surrounded by pine trees and occasional glimpses of wildlife. With the lecturer's guidance, each of us created our own individual paradise and made it as realistic as possible.

I could hear the comforting call of the birds. I could feel the warm breeze glide past me and my tiny craft. I could see the fish jumping out of the water from time to time. They seemed to have a cute little smile on their gills as they passed my boat. They were friendly little swimmers, tipping their fins as they flitted by. If they had been wearing hats (which they weren't), the hats would have been set at a jaunty angle.

Even the insects were congenial. They didn't bite or sting. They just buzzed amicably nearby, adding atmosphere to the entire panorama. I was starring in a Disney movie in my own mind. I would have burst into song if I didn't feel that it might be rude in the middle of the speaker's presentation.

I was in heaven. My body enjoyed the ambience. The scenery was gorgeous. The weather was ideal. The animals were happy. The bugs were happy. I was happy. The entire experience was peaceful and stimulating at the same time.

I was delighted.

Then, for some reason, I opened my eyes. The lights in the theatre were no longer dimmed; in fact, they were glaring. I glanced around and discovered that I was now the only person in the audience.

Apparently, I had dozed off during the lecture. The other 1,499 people got up and left to go to the next presentation on the day's agenda. None of them thought to nudge me. I probably had such an ecstatic expression on my face that they thought it best to leave me to whatever fantasy I had created for myself.

That's the whole point. After a certain age, meditation becomes just another word for "nap."

CHAPTER NINE

YOUR SUBCONSCIOUS MIND

"Honestly, sometimes I get really fed up of my subconscious—
it's like it's got a mind of its own." —Alexei Sayle

The consensus seems to be that the subconscious is the dictator of who you are, what you are, and what you will become. If you want fame, the subconscious must agree that you deserve fame. If you want fortune, the subconscious must consent. If whatever you desire doesn't coincide with what the subconscious thinks, forget about it. Your ship is sunk before it leaves the dock. That's pretty dictatorial.

On the plus side, though, if the subconscious thinks you deserve fame, it will provide it. If it feels you're worthy of wealth, the cash will flow in. Whatever you want, the subconscious will furnish, provided it believes that you are worthy of that benefit. Again, that's a potent position to hold.

But who or what is this all-powerful, all-providing force?

One expert stated that we all have but one mind—the conscious mind and the subconscious mind. Evidently, this person was not an expert in counting. However, the same person did explain that what we call the "conscious mind" and the "subconscious mind" are not really separate entities; they are separate areas of the one mind.

They perform different and discreet functions. One controls our voluntary activities; the other controls our involuntary functions. For instance, if you want to sit down, you can sit down. That's a voluntary function. Your conscious mind decides whether you sit down or don't sit down. You and your conscious mind are totally in charge of that decision. Unless, of course, someone starts singing the national anthem, then you can't sit down. However, that has nothing to do with self-improvement.

You do have many functions you must perform that are involuntary. You and your conscious mind can't control them. These are actions such as breathing, keeping your heart functioning, and a whole bunch of other stuff, most of which we're not even aware of. The subconscious controls those.

Your conscious mind doesn't tell your heart when to beat. It doesn't tell your blood how to circulate. That's a good thing—especially for us older folks—because we tend to become forgetful. Not knowing where we left the car keys or not remembering where we put our reading glasses (even when they're on top of our head) are trivial lapses. Forgetting to tell your heart when to beat can be more serious.

How does this information tie in with self-improvement? Here's a small hint—we can convert some voluntary functions to involuntary functions. As an example, I once bought a new car. The emergency brake on this new vehicle was in the center of the front seats where the gear-shifting console was. The emergency brake on my old vehicle was a pedal on the left side. For the first two or three months that I drove my new car, I would stop, shift into park, and slam my left foot on the floor . . . hard. There was no brake pedal there, but I continued to slam my foot on it anyway.

Through repetition, my mind had shifted that action from voluntary to involuntary. It was once a conscious decision that morphed into a subconscious decision.

The self-help authors tell us that we can utilize this phenomenon to improve ourselves.

Apparently, through repetition, we have forced many beliefs into our subconscious mind. The authorities tell us that these might be a hindrance to our self-improvement. As we noted earlier, the subconscious mind must approve any advancement we attempt. It can only approve if it believes we are worthy of the rewards we seek. If the subconscious doesn't support our efforts, they are doomed to failure.

Then the question is, can we consciously do anything to affect our future? The answer they tell us is that we can. We can consciously convince our subconscious to think the way we want it to think. Now the roles seemingly are reversed. Before, the subconscious controlled our thoughts; now, our conscious controls our subconscious so it controls our thoughts.

Who couldn't possibly understand this simple logic?

The subconscious has a few other traits that we can consciously benefit from.

The subconscious mind continues to work even after our conscious mind quits. We consciously stop thinking, but the subconscious continues thinking. Here's an example that you must have experienced: You are trying to recall a name that has escaped from your memory. You know the name well, but you can't seem to recall it. What most of us do is begin going through the alphabet to trigger some sort of memory response: "A . . . Adam . . . Abraham . . ." We move to "B." "Could it be Benjamin . . . Barney . . . ?" Sometimes that works; most of the time, it doesn't. Eventually, we decide trying to recall the name is not worth the exertion, so we stop. We forget about it. Then perhaps ten or twenty minutes later, with no prompting from us or our conscious mind, we shout out the name we were looking for. Why and how did it suddenly pop into our head unprompted? The answer is that while we stopped consciously trying to recall the name, our subconscious didn't. It kept searching and then produced the name.

This can be a major benefit. Often, there are projects that you are consciously working on. You might be writing a report, preparing plans, arranging a vacation—whatever. You can become weary of this task. When you tire of it, your work becomes much less efficient, less productive. You can take a break from your work. Go watch a TV show. Go for a walk. Take a nap, if you like. You can totally relax because your subconscious continues to work on that project. After you've rested and refreshed yourself, you can return to the project and you'll discover many new ideas and angles that your subconscious has graciously provided for you. You now can work more quickly and more productively. Isn't the subconscious wonderful?

Also, the subconscious mind never sleeps. We require sleep; the subconscious doesn't. You know how sometimes you like to get to the office early in the morning, before the others arrive? It seems you can get more work done without distractions and interruptions. That's how the subconscious treats sleep. It can get much more done when the conscious mind is out of its way.

We can take advantage of this. Before sleep at night, think about whatever project you're working on. Actually, tell the subconscious area of your mind that you would like solid input. Then go to sleep and don't bother it. In the morning, you may wake up with brilliant ideas that will benefit you and your project.

In any case, whether we fully understand it or not, any self-improvement program depends on coordination between the two parts of our one mind. Even though the subconscious and the conscious are one mind, there must be a communication between the two. One must give the orders, but the two probably must agree on which orders are issued. But communication and coordination are not as simple as we assume. Communication can be a complicated task. Take verbal interaction, for example. Even that seemingly easy task can become complicated.

Spoken communication goes through at least four steps. First, there is what one person actually says. Second, there is what that person thinks that he or she said. Third, there is what the second person hears and, fourth, what that person thinks he or she heard from the mouth of the first person.

When I was in school, our class went on a field trip. All of us boys wore an emblem on our shirt pockets. At one exhibit, the curator asked one of my classmates if all the students at our school were required to wear the emblem. My buddy said, "No, it's purely obligatory." That's what he said. No one had any idea what he meant to say.

One person tried to describe a film he had just seen. He felt that it was a unique movie. He said, "It was a delicate blend of the sacred and the propane." Of course, he meant to say "profane."

These illustrate that people don't always say what they are trying to say.

People don't always hear what they think they hear, either.

Once, a golfer involved in an elimination match kept saying, "I know it's winner go home." It didn't seem to make sense. In a playoff, the loser goes home and the winner continues on. Why did he keep saying that it was "winner go home"? Actually, that's what was heard, but it wasn't what he was saying. He was trying to say "win or go home." Same sound—entirely different meaning.

Once, a woman who was a liaison between a drafting office and the factory workers stormed into her supervisor's office and demanded that one of the gentlemen in the factory be disciplined. The woman was an efficient worker, often taking notes with both hands simultaneously. When the supervisor saw how furious she was, he tried to calm her. But she was adamant and claimed that she didn't have to put up with such obscenities as the factory worker had used. The supervisor met with the factory worker, the shop steward, and the offended woman. Tempers flared even more until the supervisor asked exactly what the factory worker said that was so offensive. The woman said, "He called me 'ambidextrous.'" She had heard the word correctly, but thought it meant something totally different.

Presumably, our success depends on the dialogue between the conscious and the subconscious. Dialogue, though, as we've seen, can become convoluted. Do we really want to place our future in something as faulty as communication? The following sad tale should illustrate that point:

A friend of mine was washing his car when he heard strange noises coming from the engine—which wasn't running. To investigate, he lifted the hood and startled the family cat, who somehow had snuggled atop the carburetor for a relaxing catnap. The frightened animal pounced onto my friend's head and clawed fiercely for something to hold onto. (There are surprisingly few places on the human head that offer a secure grip, by the way.)

My friend fell backward trying to free himself from the cat and stepped into the bucket of water that slipped out from under him, pitching him forward again. With one foot still in the soapy water, he landed on the engine with one hand on the positive terminal of the car's battery and the other hand on the negative terminal. He freed himself of the cat, both of his shoes, and one of his socks.

He's in the hospital now, still feeling some discomfort. He will be all right, although neither his hair nor the cat's fur will ever look the same again.

That's not the sad part, though.

That part happened when I went to visit him in the hospital. The parking lot and all the streets around the hospital had coin-operated meters. I had no change. So I parked as close to the hospital as I could in a space where the meter had expired. I planned to run in, get change for a buck, come back out, feed the meter, then go in and cheer up my smoldering friend and his new hairdo.

"Excuse me," I said to the first receptionist I saw in the hospital lobby. "Could you give me change for the parking meter?"

She never acknowledged me or the dollar, never changed her expression, never took her eyes from the computer monitor before her. "Have you ever been a patient here before?" she asked.

OK, I thought, *I can make small talk with the best of them.* "Actually, I was. It was nothing serious, but about eight months ago—"

She shoved a clipboard at me. "Fill this out."

I said, "I'd be happy to, but all I really want is—"

"Take the blue copies to Mr. McNulty in room 304. He'll stamp the yellow sheets which you'll take to Mrs. Concetti in room 403. She'll approve the pink sheets which you'll take to Mrs. Blue in 719. Mrs. Blue will issue you green sheets which you'll take to room 1222 and then take your place behind the yellow line until you're called."

"But you don't understand—"

"Next."

"You don't understand. I don't have time for all of this."

"It's the only way to check out of this hospital."

"I don't want to check out of the hospital. All I want is—"

"Why didn't you say so? Last name, please."

I said, "I don't think all this is necessary."

She barked like a drill sergeant: "Last name, please."

I gave her my last name.

She clickety-clacked on her computer keyboard and watched different information roll by on the monitor. Finally, she got one she liked. "Ah, here it is, right here," she said.

"Fine," I said and held the dollar bill out to her once again.

She took the buck and handed me a receipt. "And how will you be paying the remainder of that bill?"

I said, "What?"

She said, "You still owe $841 on your bill, Emily."

I said, "I'm not Emily, and I don't owe you any money. You owe me a dollar, and I would like to have that in two quarters, three dimes, and four nickels."

"If you can't pay now, Emily, you can arrange a partial payment schedule. Take these forms to room 703. They'll give you a yellow form which you'll then take to room 1429, in the annex, where you'll get—"

I said, "I don't want any forms of any color to take to any rooms in any building. I don't owe you any money."

"Emily, Emily, Emily," she said like a long-suffering parent. "I can't discharge you if you don't settle your bill."

I said, "I'm not a patient here. I have never been a patient here."

She said, "But you told me . . ."

"That was eight months ago. I'm not a patient now."

"But Emily, my computer says that you're in room 257."

I said, "I'm not in room 257; I'm parked outside, and I need change to put in the meter."

"But my computer says—"

"Tell your computer I'm not Emily."

She clickety-clacked on her keyboard again and said, "Oh, I see the problem. We had the last name misspelled."

"OK, fine," I said. "We all make mistakes. Now can I just have change for the parking meter?"

"We'll have to get this mix-up straightened out first. Take these pink forms to Mrs. Wilson in room 1421—that's in the annex to the annex—and she'll direct you to—"

I said, "No. Forget it. Forget everything. Keep my dollar. I'll see my buddy when he gets home. I'm leaving. I'm leaving right now."

"Not so fast, Emily." She reached over the counter and grabbed me by the shoulder. "You're not leaving this hospital without a wheelchair. Clarence, get this man a wheelchair."

I shouted, "Clarence, don't get me a wheelchair. I don't want a wheelchair. I refuse to sit in a wheelchair."

When Clarence wheeled me out into the parking lot, my car was gone.

"Where's my car?" I screamed.

The uniformed parking monitor said, "We had it towed away, sir." (At least he didn't call me "Emily.")

I asked, "Why did you tow my car away?"

He said, "The meter had expired. With you in a wheelchair and all, you should have parked in a 'handicapped' space. We have plenty of them, you know."

I said as politely and as calmly as I could, "Would you please call and get my car back?"

He said, very politely also, "I can't do that, sir. But here's the paperwork on your vehicle." He handed me about nine pieces of different-colored paper.

He said, "Just give these to the receptionist inside, and she'll tell you how you can get your car back."

I said, "Keep the car."

Now if I can't communicate well enough to get change for a dollar, should we trust our future success to a conscious mind and a subconscious mind trying to communicate intelligently with each other?

CHAPTER TEN

AUTOSUGGESTION

"I talk to myself constantly. The problem is that I rarely listen."
—Anonymous

S ince our subconscious mind controls what we really think, the real secret of self-improvement is to influence our subconscious mind. We do that by communicating with it. Since the subconscious mind is part of ourselves, we must talk to ourselves. For younger people, this one-way conversation is the gateway to success. For those of us who have attained a certain age, it's a gateway to "the home."

The consensus of those who are supposed to know is that the subconscious is the authority figure within each of us. It makes the decisions and issues the edicts. It appears to be the controlling factor of our destiny. For example, if we want to lose weight, we consciously make the decision to diet. However, if the subconscious doesn't accept our premise, then it will permit us to indulge in activities that will inhibit weight loss. It is that powerful.

Yet if the subconscious does agree with our premise of losing weight, and we continue to indulge our passion, we may continue to gain weight despite what the subconscious says or believes. So we're going to have difficulty losing weight regardless of whether the conscious or the subconscious takes charge.

Hmmm . . . forget that example.

In most cases, the subconscious dominates.

Autosuggestion is communication with our subconscious. It's an attempt to tell the subconscious what to think. Notice the apparent contradiction there—the subconscious is the supreme authority, and we're trying to control it. We're attempting to control what controls us. This entire process feels contradictory and at times, as we'll see, even shady. But to reiterate: the subconscious controls our behavior. So if we can control the subconscious, then we control our behavior. In other words, if we can control the subconscious, which is considered to be in control, then we can be in control, instead of the subconscious, which thinks it's in control. What could be simpler than that?

How do we go about telling our subconscious what to think and believe? Here are a few guiding principles:

The subconscious is extremely gullible. It acts on whatever information it receives, whether that input is valid or not . . . whether it is correct or not. It doesn't validate information it receives; it simply acts on it. For example, if you hand me a rock and tell me it's an apple, I would immediately know what you're telling me is wrong. I'm not a fool. I know the difference between a rock and an apple. And, probably, the subconscious does too. But there is a difference. You can talk until you're blue in the face, and you'll never persuade me to try to take a bite out of that rock. The subconscious is more easily deceived. If you can convince the subconscious that the rock is a juicy apple, you can run up a sizable dental bill quite quickly.

If you're walking through the woods and spot a bear dangerously close to you, your subconscious will snap into action. It will command your heart to beat faster. It will send adrenaline coursing through your body. It will respond to the danger and control your body so that it also responds.

However, if you're walking through the woods and you see a shadow that looks like a bear, your subconscious will react as if it is a bear. It will send the same signals to your heart, brain, nervous system, and whatever else so that you will behave as if it were a real, threatening bear. It's not, of course, a bear, but the subconscious, again, doesn't verify information. It accepts whatever it receives and acts accordingly, even if that information is false.

This is where the "shady" part enters. We can now try to trick our subconscious. We purposely feed it fake data so that we can benefit from it. If we're weak, we tell the subconscious we're strong, and it believes us. If we're poor, we tell the subconscious we're wealthy in the hopes that it will act on that information and give us benefits that only the wealthy are entitled to. If we're not successful, we pretend we are. The subconscious believes our sham and presents us with successful vibes and perks. We're tricking our subconscious. This feels somewhat devious.

We've become conmen who are pulling a scam on our own mind. We've taken that which is supposed to be the central authority over our well-being and turned it into a patsy, a mark, a sucker.

One suggested way to deceive our subconscious is with repetitions of affirmations. Over and over again, we tell ourselves that we are something we aren't. The classic example is the story of *The Little Engine That Could*. That locomotive kept saying, "I think I can . . . I think I can . . . I think I can." Eventually, according to the story, he could. He successfully performed his task. He's our hero.

So now we do the same thing. In effect, we lie to our subconscious. We try to convince it that we are something we're not. The theory is that a lie told often enough becomes a truth . . . especially if we keep telling it to our gullible subconscious. Anybody can fool a subconscious.

It's when this concept doesn't work that the deception becomes even more insidious. For example, you hit a terrible golf shot that sails into the woods, never to be seen again. You drop a new ball and say, "I'm a wonderful golfer. I will hit this ball far and true." *Whack*—or probably more likely *frumph*—and the ball sails only about ten yards. You hit it again, saying while swinging, "I'm a wonderful golfer. I will hit this ball far and true." You don't. You slice it into the water. You drop another ball and flail at it, saying, "I'm a wonderful golfer. I will hit this ball far and true." You swing, hear and see another disappointing splash, drop another ball, and repeat your mantra as you swing.

You've hit four bad golf shots, but you're convinced again that your next shot will be superb. You find an excuse for all the bad shots. Notice that now you're lying to yourself. You've already tried to play your subconscious for a patsy, a mark, a sucker; now you're treating yourself the same way. You're treating yourself as a patsy, a mark, and a sucker.

Your subconscious is now most likely laughing at you. It's probably saying, "Me? I have to believe what I'm told. That's how I'm built. But you? You should know better."

But we don't.

For all of the above to work, the mind must be in control. It must issue the orders, and those decrees must be obeyed. Sometimes, as years go by, the mind loses some of its dominance over the subconscious. The body begins to rebel against its subservient status. It can refuse the mind's commands for two reasons—first, sheer stubbornness, and second, decided incompetence.

The stubbornness is somewhat understandable. The body has been following orders for quite some time now. Vacations are unheard of. Promotions are nonexistent. You never hear of a body, or even a single body part, working its way up the ladder and eventually being named "mind." The caste system between mind and body is inviolate. That realization can be demoralizing to the body, and so it becomes resentful.

But the mind refuses to face the reality of many situations. It asks the body to do things it no longer is capable of doing. Whether it realizes that or not, the mind continues to issue impossible dictums. There comes a time when the body says, "I can't do that, man."

Once the mind surrenders its authority, the result is anarchy. There was a time when I was master of my domain, when I—the "I" that is the commander-in-chief of my body—was totally in charge, respected, revered, and blindly obeyed.

When, as a teenager, I played center field for the neighborhood baseball team, I'd react at the crack of the bat. "Let's go," I'd say to my body. "We can snag this fly ball."

We'd all go after it together. Arms, legs, hands, and feet would glide gracefully, with the precision and symmetry of synchronized swimmers, until we wrapped the glove around the ball effortlessly for the out.

That was back when my limbs obeyed my commands.

Of course, there were times, even as a young man, when parts of my body rebelled against other parts. For instance, there was the night my date and I left the junior prom to spend some meaningful time together in the front seat of my dad's '48 Ford. My body gleefully complied with my instructions that night until my right foot screamed, "Stop. Everybody desist. I'm caught and twisted in the glove compartment, and it's very painful. Come to my aid."

The rest of the body said, "No way, José."

The right foot yelled, "But it hurts."

The other body parts said, "We're not stopping what we're doing, because we're all having too much fun."

The foot said, "But what about me?"

They said, "You'll still be in pain when we're done doing what we're doing. We'll deal with you then."

So the right foot was democratically (and somewhat selfishly) overruled.

There have been times, too, when parts of my body did demand attention and got results. As an example, when taking a bath: One foot would step gingerly into the bath water and deliberate. "Well, the water's hot, but not too hot . . . well, I don't think it's too hot." Then that foot would call for a second opinion.

My other foot would join it in the tub, and together they'd render their judgment: "Yes, this water is all right for a bath."

When I sat down, though, other parts of the body shouted, "You two feet must be out of your mind! There's no way any of us are sitting in this liquid until it cools off a bit." Then the entire body, embarrassed feet and all, would step out of the tub and wait for the water to cool.

These instances were minor disagreements, differences of opinion. Any good leader can survive that. But today, my body is in total anarchy.

I'm playing tennis. My opponent hits the ball slightly to my right. It's a good shot, but not a great shot. Immediately, my mind reacts. It tells my body to shift to the right, bend the knees to get low to the ball, reach out with the racquet hand, and volley the ball back over the net with some force deep into the court behind my opponent. It's all very sound strategy meant to produce a decisive and impressive winning shot.

My body says, "Wait a minute. Let's think about this."

I say, "I've issued an order. Obey."

The legs say, "We are happy right where we are. If we're content right here, why should we move?"

I say, "The ball is coming—that's why we have to move. And quickly."

They say, "We moved too quickly last week, and we got a cramp. We limped for two days. We're staying where we are."

I plead, "At least bend down and try for the ball."

The knees reply, "If the legs ain't moving, we ain't bending."

The ball sailed by. I lost the point as well as the respect of my tennis partner.

This was not an isolated incident. It's been happening with some frequency. It's insurrection—and not a quiet one, either. The body is very vocal about its rebellion.

If I'm sitting comfortably and want to get up, does the body meekly comply? No. Bones creak out their dissatisfaction. Ligaments and tendons squish their displeasure. And when I do get up, all of the body parts and organs contribute to a weary sigh or sometimes a groan that seems to say, "Why did you rock the boat? We were comfortable."

It's complete anarchy.

A wise leader adjusts, though. I have. Three or four times a day now, I reassume command and bark out decisive orders.

"Listen up, body parts. We're going to take a brisk nap right now, and I don't mean maybe. I want all of you, and that means all of you, to relax and lie perfectly still. Snore if you like. But I don't want any part of this body exerting itself for any reason whatsoever without a direct command from me. Is that understood?"

"Yes, sir," they all say.

"I can't hear you," I say.

They all shout, "Yes, sir!"

And we all drift off peacefully to sleep, to nap with the precision and symmetry of a marching band. Just like in the old days.

Zzzzzzzzzz.

It's nice to be in charge again.

CHAPTER ELEVEN

MANIFESTATION

"I want to have everything . . . and then some." —Anonymous

S elf-help literature suggests that you can manifest a dream by vi-
sualizing it. Picture it intently, and it becomes reality. See and
hold any goal clearly in your mind's eye as yours, and it will
become yours. You will *manifest* that vision into your life. It's presented
that simply—if you want it, think about it, and presto! It's yours. That's
called "manifestation."

When I was a kid, I would often ask my mother for a nickel to buy
candy. Ninety-nine percent of the time, her answer was the same: "If I
had a nickel, I would sit up all night and watch it." I never could figure
out quite what she meant by that. Would she sit up all night and watch it
because she was so thrilled to have it that she couldn't be drawn away from
it? Or did it mean that she would sit up all night and watch it in order to
protect it from harm or theft? I never figured that out. One thing I always
figured out immediately was that I wasn't getting the nickel.

Now what Mom did was not manifestation. Mom didn't have to manifest the nickel; she already had it. Me? I could have visualized that nickel

all I wanted to, but I wasn't getting it. Why? Because Mom was sitting up all night watching it. That's one thing I have against manifestation. If it really worked as the self-help advocates suggest, just once I should have gotten that nickel.

We're interesting people, though. If we hear that we can get anything we want by rubbing a lamp that we find on the beach and seeing a genie pop out who will grant all of our wishes, we immediately brand that as poppycock. Yet if a self-help author tells us the exact same thing, but without the lamp and the genie, we buy into it.

That's what manifesting means. You visualize what you want, and it appears. It's yours. This is the greatest time-saving tool ever invented. If you want a hot meal, you visualize a hot meal. And it comes to you. You don't need a microwave.

You won't need a dishwasher, either. Picture the dishes and silverware as clean, and they'll be clean. This could wreak havoc on the home appliance business. It could ruin the moving companies, too. If you want to go from Wilkes-Barre, Pennsylvania, to Burlington, Iowa, with all your belongings, you just picture you, your family, and everything you own in Burlington, Iowa. Next thing you know, you, your family, and all your belongings are in Burlington. You don't damage any of your furniture, because it has remained virtually untouched. Normally, when you make a move like that, you discover when you unpack that you forgot something or lost something. Doesn't happen with manifestation. You visualize *everything* relocated to Iowa. You don't visualize everything but your favorite can opener. In order to forget something, you must purposely forget it, which is, of course, an oxymoron. You can't lose an item, because you visualized everything moved to Burlington. And, of course, if everything is moved, then you can't misplace a can opener.

It's just a wonderful invention. It's amazing that someone didn't manifest it years ago.

This is another instance in which age and experience cause skepticism. Those of us who have put a few years on our odometers tend to have seen the flaws that could be part of the theory. For instance, the process of creating what you want is never ending. Once you get what you desire, you immediately desire something else, and the process begins all over again. That, in reality, means that the process never really happened.

You don't really get what you want. You get what you thought you wanted. When you think of something better, you're no longer satisfied with what you thought you wanted before. In essence, that means you never really got what you wanted.

It's a lot like a ballplayer who is happy to be the highest-paid player in the league. But if another player comes along and signs a more lucrative contract, now the first player's not happy being the second-highest-paid player in the game. That's not what he wanted.

Getting what you want until you want something more is not really getting what you want, is it? So getting what you desire doesn't really make you happy. It makes you sad because you realize you got what you wanted but you could have gotten so much more. As a result, you got what you wanted, so you're disappointed.

Here's another dilemma we older folks might spot: The law of attraction states that if you think of something you want but don't have, it will come to you. But it also states that if you think of something you don't have and constantly think about the fact that you don't have it, then the law will grant your wish. It will allow you to continue to not have that which you think about not having. What could be clearer than that?

The irony we notice is that in order to desire something, you must admit that you don't have it. You have to concede that point. You must think that you don't have it. If you think you already have it, why would you desire it? What's to desire? You already own it. After all, let's not use this phenomenon to get greedy. But the law of attraction demands that in order to want it, you must think that you have it. In other words, in order to get what you want, you have to want what you already have. Simple, isn't it?

One book even advised that we create our own experiences. Based on that, I assume I was the one who caused me to have a flat tire while driving on the freeway. That incident cost me $120 to have the vehicle towed to a repair shop. Therefore, it seems that I'm owed $120 by . . . well, by me. It's hard to figure out how I can collect the money. Maybe I could sue. Then I would have to pay a lawyer to force me to give me 120 bucks. It hardly seems worth it, except maybe to the attorney. Come to think of it, maybe it was the attorney creating his own experiences who caused me to have a flat tire on the freeway. In that case, instead of paying him, he should reimburse me for the $120 tow fee, which I had nothing to do with creating.

Then when another idiot driver cut in front of me on the freeway, it was actually me. I created that experience, too. According to that book I was reading, I was responsible for that, also. Boy, I called myself some pretty terrible names that day.

I've got to start learning how to create better experiences.

I tried to implement the law of attraction once. I had my heart set and my thoughts focused on a specific golf club. It was a beautiful titanium driver with an enlarged sweet spot that could add thirty yards to my drives and increase my accuracy by 40 percent or more. I fantasized about that gorgeous golf club in an effort to make it mine. I wanted it to manifest like crazy. So the simplest way to make it manifest, I decided, was to buy one. However, before anything can manifest in my household, it must first survive a sophisticated defense system called "Stringent Prevention Of Unusual Spending Expenses," otherwise known as SPOUSE .

My wife said, "Tell me again. What is it you want?"

I said, "It's a new golf club. It's perfect."

She asked, "What makes it perfect?"

I said, "It has a titanium head."

"Yeah. Then what?"

I said, "A graphite shaft."

"OK. Then what?"

I said, "I don't know. A grip of some kind or another."

"Then what?"

I said, "Then nothing. Then I hold onto it and hit the ball."

She said, "Aha. I knew it had a flaw in it somewhere."

I said, "No, this club is great. All the top players use it." I showed her the pictures of the many champions who had won tournaments using this titanium driver.

She said, "You're not that good a player."

I said, "That's why I need it. To make me better."

She asked, "Buying a better golf club makes you a better player?"

I said, "Exactly."

She said, "Isn't that like trying to improve your mother's corned beef hash by buying better silverware?"

I said, "This club will make me a better golfer immediately. It's titanium, for crying out loud. That's the stuff they use for flights to the moon."

My wife said, "If going to the moon made any difference, they'd make golf clubs out of powdered orange drink ."

I said, "No. It's not the same. You're talking Tang, and I'm talking titanium."

She said, "So, titanium makes you do things better?"

I said, "Well, duh."

She said, "So, if I had bought you a titanium screwdriver, all those towel racks you put up in the bathroom would not be crooked and half hanging out of the wall?"

I said, "Titanium only helps in golf and moon landings. It's not guaranteed for do-it-yourself projects."

Now it was her turn to say, "Well, duh."

It was obvious I was getting nowhere by touting the engineering marvels of this piece of equipment. And my wife wasn't interested in how it would improve my golf game. She didn't play the game, and the only thing she liked about it was that it got me out of the house occasionally. So I tried another tack.

"This is the time to buy these clubs," I said. "They're on sale."

That got her attention. "Really? How much do they cost?" she asked.

Now I was getting somewhere.

"They're only $395," I said.

"What?!" she screamed.

I said, "I knew you'd be surprised. Isn't that a great price?"

She said, "That 'What?!' didn't mean 'What a great price!' It meant 'What fool would pay $395 for a golf stick?'"

"It's not a stick; it's a club. And it's expensive because it's titanium. All the best players are using it."

She said, "For that kind of money, Queen Elizabeth should be wearing it."

I said, "Yes, it's expensive, but golf is something that I enjoy. You have to spend money on the things you enjoy."

She said, "I enjoy talking to my parents on the phone every once in a while."

"I know that," I said.

"But every time I call them long distance, you put an egg timer by my elbow."

(That was a very strategic play on her part.)

I said, "OK, you can call them while I'm out buying the club. Talk as long as you want."

"Oh, that's a great deal," she said. "You get a $400 golf club and I get one phone call."

I reminded her, "You can talk as long as you want."

She said, "I'd have to talk for 6,000 minutes to break even."

I said, "Honey, I really, really want this golf club."

She said, "Let me get this straight. You want to spend $400 to buy a golf club that you don't really know how to use so you can hit a $2 ball somewhere where you can't even find it?"

"But, Honey, I love golf, and this will improve my game."

She said, "If I recall, you ranted and raved when I wanted to spend $150 to buy myself a new party dress."

"Yeah, but you have a closet full of dresses."

"And what's in your golf bag? Chicken wings?"

Well, I was a big smash the next time I played golf with the guys.

"Wow, that's a new club, isn't it?" my playing partner asked.

"Yeah," I said.

"What kind is it?"

I told him, "It's the new titanium driver."

"Graphite shaft?"

"Oh, yeah."

"Do you like it?"

"I love it. It adds thirty yards to my drives."

"That'll get you almost up to 150 yards," they teased.

"Very funny," I said.

"No, it's nice. How much did it cost?"

"A little under $900," I said.

"Wow. That's pretty expensive, isn't it?"

"Not really," I said. "It was $395 for the club and about $400 for a couple of dresses for the wife."

"That's not $900."

"And a $100 phone call to tell her mother all about her new clothes."

So be careful when manifesting. It can cost an arm and a leg. And, incidentally, my drives didn't go any farther, and they certainly didn't go any straighter. But I did march into the woods looking for the ball with my head held high and my chest swollen with pride. I was carrying a golf bag that had a genuine titanium driver in it.

I manifested it myself.

CHAPTER TWELVE

SINGLENESS OF PURPOSE

"Obstacles are those frightful things you see when you
take your eyes off your goal." —Henry Ford

There are two factors that are essential to achieving any goal—
focus and singleness of purpose. They're similar but with an
essential difference: Focus means concentrating intently on
what you're doing at the moment. Singleness of purpose means that you
are always concentrating on one thing—that which you want to achieve.

These two are different in that one is a specialized form of the other. It's
like saying that all kangaroos are animals, but not all animals are kangaroos. The kangaroo is one specific animal. Here's an example:

Consider a child in the classroom. She is gazing out the window at a
glorious, beautifully colored bird. This young student is fascinated with
this bird. She focuses on the colors and the song of this unique creature.

However, she does this while the teacher is discoursing on the finer points of the Pythagorean theorem (assuming that the Pythagorean theorem has finer points). That's this young girl's goal for the day: to learn the Pythagorean theorem so that she'll be able to use it in her later life. Now, you and I know that the Pythagorean theorem states that $c^2 = a^2 + b^2$. We're aware of that because of the many times we've used it in our own daily lives. But this schoolchild doesn't know it and probably won't learn it today because she has taken her mind off of the primary goal of learning that theorem and is focusing on the fascinating study of the bird outside her classroom window. She is focusing, but not on the primary goal, not on the singleness of purpose.

Let's take another example: the legendary race between the tortoise and the hare. The smart money that day was on the hare. Everyone knew that the hare was much faster than the tortoise and that it wouldn't really be a contest at all. Everyone conceded that—except for the tortoise. The tortoise was focused on winning that race. Of course, the hare was also.

The hare naturally shot out to a commanding, seemingly insurmountable lead. The tortoise simply plodded forward as best it could. But then the hare made a fatal mistake. It took its eye off the ultimate goal. It abandoned its focus on the finish line. It gave up on that singleness of purpose.

While the rabbit took a nap by the side of the road, the tortoise remained focused on the primary goal, passed the sleeping hare, and trudged across the finish line, winning the race.

It almost wiped out several Las Vegas betting rooms and more than a few local bookies. And there have been some rumors that the tortoise did in fact call Uber or flag down a cab to make up some of the lead. Those are all unconfirmed conspiracy theories, though. The fact remains that the speedier hare lost the race because it lost that singleness of purpose.

Somewhere along the line, a brief nap was more important than crossing the finish line.

Napoleon Hill calls this singleness of purpose "having a definite purpose in life." It requires such focus that nothing can replace it. It must be the prime focus that encompasses all other focuses in your life. Notice in the

fable above how the hare surrendered that primary goal to a lesser goal—
the brief respite. That one error in judgment cost the furry, fleet-footed
bunny the prize.

There's nothing wrong with taking a short slumber when you're tired.
That's sensible. But it can be a dreadful mistake when you lose sight of the
ultimate goal and, eventually, lose the ultimate prize.

Napoleon Hill and many of the self-help experts who followed advised
us that singleness of purpose should become an obsession if we want to
achieve a goal—any goal. Our focus should remain exclusively on that objective. No other activity (like a brief nap) should interfere. So to keep our
eyes on the prize, we should ask three questions about any options we
may have:

1. Will this other activity aid me in accomplishing my definite
   chief purpose in life? (If it will, do it.)

2. Will this other activity hinder me in accomplishing my definite
   chief purpose in life? (If it will, don't do it.)

3. Will this other activity have no bearing one way or the other on
   accomplishing my definite chief purpose in life? (If that's true,
   then do whatever you want.)

Nevertheless, even in doing whatever you want, you should maintain
focus.

"Focus" is another way of saying "Anything that's worth doing is worth
doing well." Focusing on any chore builds the habit of doing things well.
Being true to our dedication to things that are neutral is excellent training
for being meticulous in those things that are designed to help us achieve
our goal. If the hare had always finished his races even when he was merely
in training, today he would have an extra trophy in his den. And the tortoise would have one less.

If we're trying to achieve a goal, we should focus and try to do our best
in any endeavor, but especially in those that lead directly to our definite
chief purpose in life. Again, we hit a problem when we consider that focus
is easier for the young than it is for the more mature.

Many of us older folks get up with a definite purpose and go into another room, presumably to fulfill whatever that purpose was. When we get there, we forget what we went there for. We not only take our eyes off the ultimate prize—we totally forget what in tarnation we're doing. We'd be happy to focus on whatever it is we wanted to do when we start doing it, but we can't start doing it because we can't remember what it was we wanted to do. As the proverbial saying goes, "The spirit is willing, but the mind seems to have gone to another country."

Once again, wise and beneficial self-help principles fail the older generation. We find it challenging to focus on anything—at least for very long. Some of us can bend over to tie a loose shoelace and then suddenly wonder what we're doing bent over like this. My grandfather once tried to repair a watch for me. It was the old windup type of wristwatch, and I loved that thing. I wanted that thing to work so badly, and Grandpop knew that and volunteered that we fix it together.

Although Grandpop did all the work, I was so proud to be working alongside him and pretending to help. Together we took that thing apart, cleaned and oiled it, then reassembled it. Well, we reassembled most of it. Grandpop forgot to put back two parts—the hour hand and the minute hand.

The watch worked perfectly, but it couldn't tell time. And I could never tell Grandpop.

Singleness of purpose requires focus. It is a specialized form of focus. As we said before, it is focusing on your definite chief purpose in life—your ultimate prize. But it's difficult after a certain age to keep your mind concentrating on whatever you want to achieve when you have trouble concentrating on anything at all or even remembering what it was that you should have been concentrating on.

It's frustrating and annoying, and not only to us but often to others as well.

Not too long ago, my wife came home from shopping, which she normally does on Thursdays. I helped her in with the bags of groceries, which I normally do. She then asked if there were any messages, which she normally does. I said, "Oh, yeah, there was. Your friend . . . uh . . . June called."

My wife said, "You mean 'Joan'?"

"Yeah. Joan. Isn't that what I said?"

"You said 'June.'"

I said, "Well, I meant 'Joan.'"

My wife said, "So?"

I said, "So she called."

My wife said, "Well, what did she call about?"

"Oh . . . I see what you mean. Her daughter, Sally . . ."

My wife corrected me again. "Sarah."

"Yeah, Sarah, June's daughter."

"Joan's daughter."

I said, "Right. She had her baby."

"Really?"

I said, "Yeah."

My wife was excited.

I said, "Everybody's fine."

My wife said, "That's wonderful. Did she have a boy or a girl?"

I said, "Yes."

My wife persisted. "Well, what was it—a boy or a girl?"

I confessed. "I'm a little fuzzy on that."

My wife said, "How can you be fuzzy? It has to be either a boy or a girl."

I said, "I already agreed to that."

"Well, what was it?"

I said, "It was a boy . . . I think."

My wife stared at me in disbelief with a soupçon of annoyance. "You think?"

I said, "Yeah, I think. She told me what it was, but I'm not sure now."

"You're not sure?"

"No. I forget."

Now my wife resorted to sarcasm. She said, "It's not like she gave birth to a butterfly where there are 165,000 different species. She either had a boy or a girl. Which one was it?"

"I can't recall which of the two it was. I was watching the ball game at the time, and it was a really good game. Listen to this . . . the Cowboys were losing in the last quarter . . ."

My wife wasn't interested in what had distracted me. She said, more calmly now, "What was the baby's name? That should give us a clue."

I said, "That's great thinking. The name will certainly help."

"Well, what was it?" she asked.

I said, "Jennifer."

My wife said, "Well, there. Then the baby must be a . . ."

". . . or Jonathan or something like that."

My wife glared at me. I saw the anger in her eyes and, I think, tiny little puffs of smoke coming out of her ears. She said, "Or something like that?!"

"I'm pretty sure it began with a 'J.'" I was proud of myself for remembering that detail—despite how close the game was.

My wife said, "So the name could be Julie . . . or John . . . ?"

"Could be," I said. "I'm not really certain."

My wife wouldn't let up. "Or it could be Jambalaya . . . or Juicemaker . . . or Juxtaposition . . ."

I said, "None of those sound familiar."

My wife threw some sort of cooking implement across the kitchen.

I said, "Control yourself, Honey. It's just a name."

"No, it's not 'just a name,'" she said. "It's a letter of the alphabet. It could be any one of 165,000 names."

"The same as the number of butterflies." I tried to joke, but she had none of it.

"This is not funny," she pointed out.

"But it's not a catastrophe," I observed.

My spouse just glared at me, giving me the distinct impression that she thought it was a catastrophe.

I said, "Look, you're going to call Whatshername to congratulate her anyway, aren't you?"

She said, "Of course."

I said, "Well, when you do, just ask her if the baby was a boy or a girl and ask what his or her name is."

"I can't do that," she said.

"Why not?"

She said, "I'd be too embarrassed."

I said, "Why?"

My wife explained, "When someone calls and tells you about a new baby, you always ask if everyone is all right."

"I did that."

"Congratulations," she said with no sincerity. "And you find out if it's a boy or a girl and what the baby's name is."

I said, "You can't ask that stuff later?"

She said, "That would be gauche."

I said, "Wait a minute. You mean if someone calls and tells you about a new baby and you don't catch the baby's name, you have to go through the rest of your life not knowing what the kid is called?"

She said, "You should have cared enough to ask."

"I did ask," I insisted.

"Then you should have cared enough to remember," she insisted in return.

"I'm sorry," I said, "But she called at a bad time. I was half listening to her and half watching the end of the game on TV."

"Your stupid game was more important than a message from my best friend?"

"No, it wasn't more important, just more exciting. You see, Dallas was down by 11 with just 2:31 remaining. They scored a touchdown with 1:57 left in the game, so they decided to go for the two-point conversion. That would put them within a field goal of a tie. But they didn't make it, so now they needed a touchdown. A field goal wouldn't do them any good. The onside kick was unsuccessful, but Buffalo fumbled on third down with just 47 seconds remaining. Dallas started driving, and then—"

My wife said, "You can remember all of this but you can't remember whether the woman on the phone said whether it was a boy or a girl."

"Right. But let me tell you how the game ended . . ."

"I don't care how the stupid game ended. The next time you take a call about a birth announcement, you find out the sex of the baby, the name of the baby, and how much the baby weighs."

I said, "Uh-oh."

"How much did the baby weigh?" she asked.

"I think it was like six, seven, or eight pounds. Somewhere in that area."

"Get out of my sight," she recommended.

I followed her recommendation. I went over to the club and played some cards with the guys.

One pal of mine said, "You're not playing very well. You seem a little distracted."

"Yeah," I said. "I am."

He said, "What's the problem?"

I said, "I had a little dispute with the wife."

He asked, "Over what?"

I said, "Damned if I know."

And Napoleon Hill and his buddies expect a scatterbrain like me to keep my mind focused on my definite chief purpose in life?

CHAPTER THIRTEEN

DO THE WORK

"Doing nothing is difficult. You never know when you're done."
—Anonymous

R etirement is wonderful. It's a chance to do nothing all day and not worry about getting caught at it. It's glorious freedom from deadlines, performance, responsibilities, reporting to work on time, trying to get the office clock to move faster when it's nearing quitting time, and being civil to an uncivil boss. It's wonderful.

In your retirement, you can stay up late because you don't have to get up in the morning. Of course, if you want to, you can get up early. As a retiree, you can get up anytime you want and as often during the day as you want. You can wake up in the early morning and you can wake up again in the late morning. You can wake up right before lunch and again right after lunch. You can wake up midday, again before dinner, maybe even after dinner. Some dedicated nappers may even wake up during dinner.

Of course, retirement is not necessarily wonderful for those around you. One day, I announced to my wife, "I'm not going to play golf today."

She said, "Yes, you are."

She called and arranged my tee time and also got me three others to form my foursome. She just wanted me out of the house. It annoyed her that I was retired and could sleep away most of my waking hours. She rightly believed that there was no retirement from cooking, cleaning, doing laundry, and other household tasks.

I sympathized with her. She was living with a person who insisted on doing nothing. Even when we traveled together, one of us did nothing. Once I got to a hotel room, I could see no good reason to leave. I'd lie down on the bed, begin my nap, and never really end it until the vacation was over.

My wife claims that traveling with me is like traveling with an extra duffel bag. You haul it up to the room, toss it on the bed, and it just lies there.

This is what we've all been working toward—not working. Doing nothing. Now, some people will say, "Well, now that you're retired, you should take up golf. You should get interested in gardening. You might even take some lessons and start painting. You could go fishing." They offer all sorts of activities that you'll now have time for. It's an oxymoronic idea that says that now that you've got nothing to do, you've got plenty of time to do something. It's like the gentleman who once said, "I'd give my right arm to be ambidextrous."

Here's something you well might read in a self-improvement volume:

Sit in a comfortable chair with your feet flat on the floor and your hands relaxed, either on the arms of the chair or on your lap. Picture yourself on a balmy beach. See the beautiful cloud formations floating slowly overhead. See the seagulls gliding gracefully in the sky. Listen to the soothing sounds of the ocean. Watch the waves breaking over one another and drifting comfortably back to the sea. Feel the sun warming your face. Feel the occasional sea breeze blowing over your body. Allow your entire body to relax. Feel the muscles in your shoulders go limp. Let the tension drain out of your arms, your hands, your fingers. Your legs and your feet grow more and more comfortable. Your entire body is free of pressure. Your mind is content to think of nothing except the pure relaxation of your surroundings.

That's something that the self-help author might offer to aid you in achieving your goals. However, what are you doing while you're following these instructions? What is your image doing as it sits contentedly on this beach? It's doing absolutely nothing. So the self-helpers are telling you that you can do something by doing nothing.

There's nothing wrong with doing nothing. In fact, it has benefits. For instance, you can't get bitten by a dog while doing nothing. Well, perhaps you can, but you wouldn't if the dog had been doing nothing.

You can't fall down a flight of stairs doing nothing. You can fall out of your chair, but after a certain age, we all do that.

Road rage would be nonexistent. If someone cuts you off on the freeway, do nothing. There's no road rage. In fact, you shouldn't be on the freeway at all. You should be home in your chair actively doing nothing.

Wouldn't the world be a wonderful place if people would just stay in their dens and do nothing? There would be no problems. All problems in the world today begin with someone doing something. If nobody did anything, who would we get mad at?

Therein lies the flaw with all self-help advice—it requires you to do something.

There's no escape from it. If you want to achieve something, you have to do something. Years ago, an advertising slogan was quite popular. It suggested that you could learn whatever it is they were selling "in ten easy lessons." One comic of that day made fun of it. He said, "Learn to play piano in ten easy lessons . . . or three very, very hard ones."

There was wisdom in his jest. He was pointing out the obvious—that to do anything, you have to do something. You want to learn to juggle, you have to practice juggling. You want to be a world-class ice skater, you have to get on the ice and fall on your bottom a few times. You want to advance at work, you have to learn more or work harder. You have to do something.

Often, the self-help literature keeps this fact hidden. They imply that just reading the book will be enough. It isn't. And, in fact, once you read the book and apply its principles, you may discover that they don't really work. What do the authors say then? They say that the principles weren't effective because you didn't do them well enough. We're back to the oxymoronic idea—with this book, you don't have to do anything, but if you don't do it, it won't work.

Try reading a book about driving and then, with no experience, taking the family car out for a spin on the interstate during rush hour. You'll wind up with someone else's fender sitting in the passenger seat.

Try climbing into a boxing ring and facing a vicious foe with nothing to back you up except the aspirations from *The Little Engine that Could*: "I think I can, I think I can, I think I can." After your opponent lands the first left hook, that mantra will quickly change to "I think I'm unconscious, I think I'm unconscious, I think I'm . . ."

With all of the self-improvement literature, you have to do something. They should come with warnings written on the cover: "Some assembly required" or "Success not included."

Regardless of the self-help advice offered, you are required to take action. The suggestions are useless without preparation, study, and practice. That's why doctors hang diplomas on their office walls—to prove that they completed the requirements.

The literature promotes this "do nothing" concept. If they don't come out and promise it, they do imply it. Several of the books suggest that you can acquire whatever you think about. They almost guarantee that if you think about a goal long enough, hard enough, and consistently enough, you will achieve it. Well, during my middle school and high school years, I thought about nothing but girls. I still wound up taking my cousin to the senior prom.

He was more embarrassed than I was.

When I was a kid, I learned that a line was the shortest distance between two points. We were told in school that this was axiomatic. After I looked up "axiomatic," I still didn't accept it. I spent a good deal of my time desperately trying to find a shortcut between those two points. It was fruitless, naturally. It's just as pointless to try to find a shortcut to self-improvement. Achievement requires diligent activity. If you want to be rich, famous, or powerful, you're going to have to take some steps to become more rich, famous, or powerful. Despite what the literature may guarantee, there are no shortcuts.

But no; we want shortcuts. We expect to learn to play the guitar without practicing forming the chords. We want to read a book about gymnastics and expect that we will do a tumbling run with flips and leaps and turns, all without ever getting our bodies limber enough to flip, leap, or turn.

There was a time when I wanted to improve my life and was willing to do the work. My wife is wiser than I. She insisted that the spirit may be willing, but often the flesh (especially my flesh) is weak. The dispute began with my wife saying, "Oh no you don't." She didn't yell it, but it seemed loud because it startled me. I was innocently reading at the time. "What?" I said. "I'm not doing anything."

"And let's keep it that way."

I had no idea what she was talking about, so I told her that. "I have no idea what you're talking about," I said.

She said, "I found an 800 number written on a slip of paper by the telephone."

I said, "Where should I keep 800 numbers? By the washer-dryer?"

She said, "We're not buying another album from some washed-up country singer."

I said, "I still don't know what you're talking about."

She said, "You're going to buy another of those song collections that are 'not available in record stores.' Don't you know they're not available in record stores because if they put them in record stores, nobody would buy them?"

I told her, "It's not a CD. I'm buying something else I saw on television."

She said, "Please don't. We either don't need it or it won't work when we get it."

I said, "It's a set of exercise tapes to get me back in shape again."

"That's different," she said. "That falls under both categories."

I said, "Honey, I want to shape up and slim down. I want to get back to my original weight."

She said, "Eight pounds, four ounces?"

I said, "You know what I mean—the weight I was when I was young and athletic."

She said, "You want to have abs of steel and buns of steel?"

"Those aren't the tapes," I said. "But, yes, that's what I want."

"You don't need them," she said. "I like you just the way you are—abs of flab and seat of meat."

"See . . . that's what I mean," I said.

She said, "I'm only kidding."

I said, "I know, but wouldn't you like to have a husband with abs and buns of steel?"

She said, "Sure. Then I could hang messages on you with refrigerator magnets."

I said, "You can laugh all you want, but I'm going to get these tapes and whip myself into shape."

She said, "Honey, you know they never work."

I had her there. "They have to work," I told her. "They guarantee that after seven weeks, you will have lost four inches off your waist."

She said, "And I guarantee that after seven weeks, you will not have played these tapes for six."

"What do you have against these tapes?" I asked.

"How much do they cost?"

I said, "If I act now, I can get the complete series of four tapes for only $69.95."

She said, "That's what I have against them."

I had her again. "Actually, I'll be saving money. Once I slim down, I'll be able to fit into clothes that I haven't worn in years."

She said, "Honey, I hate to tell you this, but those clothes went out of style two years before you stopped wearing them."

Now the discussion was getting a little personal and vindictive. She was hitting below my abs of steel—or future abs of steel.

I said, "Honey, I'm ordering those tapes. I'm going to work out every day, and you'll see that I do have willpower; soon, you'll be looking at a new man."

"When are you going to work out?" she asked.

I said, "I'll get up early every morning."

She said, "You already get plenty of exercise in the morning—reaching over time and time again to hit the snooze button on your alarm clock."

"That was the old me," I explained.

"The old you, the new you, or the middle-aged you—none of that group will work out to these tapes."

I said, "You're sure of that?"

She said, "I'm positive of that. These tapes may be wonderful and effective and may work miracles, but they only do those things if you do the work that they require."

I said, "I'll do whatever work they ask me to do."

She said, "Then how come you never do the work that I ask you to do?"

I said, "Like what?"

She said, "Like fix the broken screen door in the back of the house." She said, "Like fix the leaky faucet in the upstairs bathroom." She said, "Like fix the lights in the backyard."

I said, "All that light needs is a new bulb."

"But someone has to put that bulb in, and apparently neither the old you, the new you, or whatever 'you' you were in between is going to do that. And incidentally it's not 'that light'; it's 'those lights.' There are fourteen lights around the backyard, and twelve of them don't work."

"I'll get around to it."

"That's exactly what you'll say after you stop doing the exercises on these tapes: 'I'll get around to it.' I'm betting you won't 'get around to it.'"

"I will," I said with determination.

She conceded defeat. "All right. Order the tapes if you insist. But I want $10 a week added onto my shopping allowance."

"Why?" I asked.

She said, "If you're going to try to develop abs of steel and buns of steel, you're going to need plenty Ben of Gay."

I did order the tapes. Did I do the workouts faithfully as I vowed, or did I abandon them after a few days of faux dedication? I'll leave that to your imagination. But I will give you a hint: if you ever want to buy some workout tapes at an extraordinarily low price, drop me a line.

CHAPTER FOURTEEN

GO THE EXTRA MILE

"There are no traffic jams along the extra mile."
—Roger Staubach

This is the story of two neighbors who were working on home improvement projects. Each of them was redesigning the garage in the front of his house. Both of them were competent builders. Their homes were similar in size and status. The neighborhood was well manicured, and all of the houses were kept in good repair. Both of them had approval from the city authorities for the work they were doing. One man, though, went about his work somewhat grudgingly, while the other worked happily, exuberantly.

Occasionally, the neighbors would stop and talk with the workers as they labored.

"What sort of job are you doing, Hank?" (Hank was the disgruntled one.)

"Aw, I gotta redo the garage. The dumb builders didn't make it big enough. Our car just about fits in here."

"Well, they have made cars larger lately."

"Yeah, well, the contractors should have thought of that. Besides, there's not enough storage space. The place looks like a junk shop."

"Maybe while you're at it, you could build in a nice series of cabinets. You can cram an awful lot of storage into a small space that way."

"I got enough problems just getting the job done. My wife's always coming up with new ideas. 'This is not good enough.' 'This is not big enough.' 'This is not the way I wanted it.' I don't need new projects to add onto it now."

"I just thought that while you've got it torn down, that would be a good time to add the improvements."

"I don't want to improve it. I just want to get it finished."

"Well, if it's any consolation, it's looking pretty good."

"Well, that's not much consolation, because it's not finished. It'll look good when it's just sitting out here and I'm inside taking a nap. That's when it'll look good."

"Well, good luck with it. And remember I have a bunch of tools. And you're welcome to them. Don't hesitate to ask."

"Why don't you bring a couple of those tools down and help me finish this thing so I can get out from under this project?"

"OK, Hank, I'll talk to you later. Say hello to Marge for me."

"Marge and I aren't talking."

The neighbor continued on his way, and Hank slammed more two-by-fours into place, hammered them aggressively, and cursed when they didn't fit snugly. He would finish the enlargement of his garage, but he would resent it and the anguish it caused him. He and his garage would never live happily ever after.

Gary, the other do-it-yourselfer, followed the example of the seven dwarfs. He whistled while he worked. In fact, he outdid the dwarfs. He would hum and sometimes sing out with gusto. It was still somewhat annoying, but better than Hank's constant complaining. The neighbors, in fact, chuckled at the lively cheerfulness that Gary brought to his hammering and sawing.

"Are you enlarging your garage, too, Gary?" a passing neighbor asked.

"No, my friend, I'm not. It is where the garage used to be, and it may look like I'm enlarging that space, but actually, I'm working toward a much loftier goal."

"Really? What goal is that?"

"I'm laboring as the stone masons and architects of the Middle Ages did. In my mind and heart, I'm actually building a cathedral."

"Wow! That is lofty."

"And uplifting, my good man. My spirits soar heavenward with each nail I drive. My soul sings with each patch of cement that I smooth out. My heart is carried aloft as I see the spires of this great basilica stretching towards the clouds."

"You have an admirable imagination."

"And it serves me well. This is not a labor to me; it's a joy. It's a contribution to my home, to my neighborhood, and to the entire world."

"Boy, I'd like to hire you sometime to help me mow the lawn and put the trash out."

"Just do all chores with joy, my good man, all chores with joy. Hi-ho, hi-ho, it's back to work I go . . ."

The neighbor continued his stroll, and Gary continued his happy work.

Both men finished their projects. Hank's passed inspection with no problem at all. The homeowner's association, though, had a problem with Gary's garage. When the representatives came to visit Gary, they admitted the stained glass windows were a conversation piece and a tourist attraction in the neighborhood, but having the bells in the steeple chime every hour on the hour was starting to annoy the neighbors.

Admittedly, Gary brought extra enthusiasm to his home improvement project. He genuinely attempted to go the extra mile. Perhaps he went a little too far. That's one of the drawbacks of going the extra mile—after you go that mile, should you go another mile? Another half a mile? Another quarter of a mile? Whatever happened to the good old-fashioned honest day's work for an honest day's pay? Whatever became of getting what you paid for? When did we start expecting to get what we paid for plus a little bonus that we didn't pay for—the extra mile?

Two couples went out to dine together frequently. They had a favorite restaurant that they would visit regularly—once a week or once every two weeks. They became good friends with the owner. One night after finishing their meals, the owner served each of them an after-dinner cordial. No charge. It was a sweet-tasting, "go the extra mile" bonus. They enjoyed it and expressed their appreciation.

The owner continued this nicety for several of their visits thereafter. Then one night, after dinner, one of the gentlemen said, "Instead of Grand Marnier tonight, I'd prefer a taste of Drambuie." The owner billed them for their cordials that evening. The patrons mentioned that, normally, these drinks were complimentary. Why were they being billed this evening?

The owner explained that the establishment does that for certain favored customers—which they were—but only for a certain amount of time. Certainly not in perpetuity. The customers were offended and vowed never to eat in this restaurant again. And they never did.

So, if you go the extra mile, you'd better be prepared to keep on going with it.

Napoleon Hill was a great believer in going the extra mile. He recommended it in his books, and many readers followed his advice and benefited from it. Certainly, going that extra mile is admirable and commendable for those who have some extra miles left in their tank. Many of us, though, have traveled many miles in our journey through life and we must conserve those few miles that we may have left. I, for one, don't relish going an extra mile. I don't even like to leave the house. In fact, it requires a certain effort even to leave the couch some days.

I will use as much ingenuity today to avoid going *any* miles as I used to expend years ago when trying to impress and succeed. One of my useful devices is to plead ignorance. The following tale illustrates my cleverness:

My wife said, "You'd better start getting ready. We have to be there in an hour."

"Be where?" I asked.

"We're going to a cookout at Martha and Charles's place tonight."

"I'm not going anywhere tonight," I said.

"We have to go," my wife insisted. "I told them we'd be there."

"You may have told them, but you never told me."

"I did tell you," she told me.

"Did not."

"Did."

I explained quite logically, "If you had told me, I would have known about it. Since I don't know about it, you obviously didn't tell me."

She said, "The problem is that you never listen to me when I tell you something. From now on, when I tell you something, I'm going to demand a written receipt."

"Do you have a receipt now?" I asked.

She said, "No."

"See. You didn't tell me."

She said, "You do this to me every time."

"Oh, now it's all my fault because you never told me we were going out tonight."

"You ask me everyday what we're having for dinner. I tell you. An hour later, you ask me again, then you ask me again and again."

"That's malarkey," I said. "If you tell me what we're having for dinner, why would I keep asking over and over again?"

"OK," she said smugly, "What are we having for dinner tonight?"

I looked puzzled.

She rubbed it in. "Come on, Mr. I-Remember-Everything-You-Tell-Me, what am I making for dinner tonight?"

I confessed. "I don't know."

She said, "I'm not making anything for dinner tonight. We're going to a cookout tonight at Martha and Charles's."

"We are?"

"Yes. I just told you about it."

"Well, you should have told me earlier."

"I did tell you earlier!" she shouted.

"I don't think you did," I said calmly.

"You never remember anything I tell you. You really should have that checked."

"Have what checked?"

"Your memory."

I said, "That's nonsense. I have a mind like a . . . a . . . steel . . . uh . . ."

"Steel trap," she hinted.

"Yeah. Like a steel trap. That's what I was trying to think of."

"See that?" she said. "You don't even know what you have a mind like unless I tell you."

"Well, you didn't tell me we were going out tonight."

"I did," she insisted. "And you'd better start getting ready."

"But I was going to stay home tonight and watch the big boxing match."

"Well, tonight we're going to be at a cookout at Martha and Charles's. I told them we'd be there."

"You told them, but you never told me."

"Yes, I did. Now go get ready."

"But this is the big match. It's between Whatshisname and some other famous guy."

"You've got that steel trap working again, huh?" She loves sarcasm.

"Well I don't remember their names, but I know I'd rather watch the fight than go to . . . whose place are we going to again?"

She said wisely (and she was right), "You're just doing this to try to get out of going. Go get dressed."

So I showered and dressed for an exciting cookout at Martha and Charles's. We had to go because they were expecting us to be there and all their friends were expecting us to be there. Everyone was expecting us to be there except for me. I didn't expect to be there because no one told me I was expected to be there.

My wife still maintained that she had told me.

In any case, we arrived, and Martha and Charles greeted us warmly.

"Glad you could make it," Charles said.

"Are you kidding?" I said. "I've been looking forward to this for weeks."

Charles asked, "Can I get you anything?"

I said, "A cold iced tea would be nice, and maybe you could turn the TV on and we can catch a little bit of the big boxing match."

Charles said, "You mean the one between Whatshisname and the famous guy?"

I said, "I'd like to see a little bit of that."

He said, "That was on last night."

I said, "Really? Nobody told me."

He said, "It was a great fight."

I asked, "Did you watch it?"

He said, "Of course."

I said, "Who won?"

He said, "I forget."

I was beginning to like Charlie a little bit more. He was learning to use the *forgetfulness gambit* to get out of leaving the house, too.

Anybody can use this ploy. Most likely, Napoleon Hill in his later years often *forgot* to go the extra mile.

CHAPTER FIFTEEN

AVOID PROCRASTINATION

"Procrastination is the art of keeping up with yesterday."
—Don Marquis

This chapter obviously deals with procrastination. To get the full effect of it, you probably shouldn't read it until tomorrow . . . or maybe the day after. As Mark Twain once quipped, "Never put off until tomorrow what you can do the day after tomorrow." Mark Twain probably lived by that philosophy, and yet he managed to achieve a fair level of prominence.

Yet the self-improvement advocates treat this subject as a disabling disease. They abhor the idea of putting things off. What is it that makes today so much more appealing to them than tomorrow?

Listen to a few of their quotes:

"Procrastination is opportunity's assassin." —Victor Kiam

"Procrastination is the thief of time." —Edward Young

"What may be done at anytime will be done at no time."
—Scottish proverb

"The best way to get something done is to begin." —Unknown
(The author probably was going to put his name after this quote
but never got around to it.)

"Procrastination is like trying to get rich by betting on the winning horse the day after the race has been run." —Author either
unknown or unwilling to own up to it

Notice the obsession with today. It's almost as if tomorrow doesn't
exist. It's a Cinderella syndrome. When the midnight hour tolled, everything that existed today disappeared. Her coach turned back into a
pumpkin. The footmen turned back into rodents. Her gorgeous gown
returned to tatters. Everything dematerialized. Her fairy godmother had
superpowers that could instantly create all these luxuries, but she wasn't
powerful enough to get a one-hour extension so that Cinderella could get
safely home.

That's what we're taught about procrastination. Imagine if Alexander
Fleming had been working on discovering penicillin but took a coffee
break because it was getting late. While he was adding the sugar and cream
to his coffee, the day ended. It was two minutes past midnight, and he was
prepared to add the finishing touches to this medical breakthrough. "Too
late!" the antiprocrastinators shouted. "You should not have put it off so
long. Now the world will never have this wonderful miracle drug."

How about if Alexander Graham Bell had put off placing that histor-
ic first phone call to Thomas Watson until the next day? He might have
gotten this response: "Your call is very important to us, but since the telephone has not been invented yet, we are not in a position to accept it.
Please reinvent the phone and call at a later time." All of the iPhones you
see today would not be here because of procrastination.

How about the Wright brothers? Suppose on December 17, 1903, Orville had called Wilbur and said, "Wil, the wife wants to go Christmas shopping today. How about if I meet you at Kitty Hawk sometime tomorrow and we'll get that plane up in the air?" If that had happened, business people all over the country would be walking to their meetings in Chicago and security agents in airports all across the world would be unemployed. All because of procrastination.

All of the wonderful luxuries that enhance our lives—televisions, microwave ovens, cordless razors, remote control devices, automobiles, thermos bottles—might not exist if they had been postponed until tomorrow.

What is so precious about today? Why is it so unyielding? Suppose the Duke of Wellington gathered his troops together and said to them on June 18, 1815, "Hey guys, we've had a long day. Why don't you all get a good night's rest and be up bright eyed and bushy tailed first thing in the morning, and we'll get the battle started?" Would Napoleon still have lost at Waterloo?

What is it about today that has such appeal for the self-help crowd? If you ran into your own fairy godmother and she promised you wealth, fame, and power starting tomorrow, would you turn it down because she couldn't make it available today? Probably not.

They say that "tomorrow never comes." It's not true. If that were true, wouldn't the reverse apply? If tomorrow never comes, doesn't that mean that yesterday never existed?

It's interesting that self-improvement advocates are antiprocrastination yet they recommend so much planning. Make a to-do list for today. Lay out your short-term goals. Project your long-term goals. They expect you to figure out what you're going to accomplish in five or ten years but expect you to finish it today. If today is so dreadfully important, why do they have calendars with all the other days printed on them?

I'm actively pro-procrastination. (I should come up with a better term for that, but I can always do it later.) My wife sometimes asks me why I nap so much. I explain that I have put off so many things until tomorrow that I have to rest up today in order to get them all done. I find procrastination easy. Once you put everything off until tomorrow, you can take the rest of the day off. So I do.

I belong to a very active Procrastinator's Club. We meet on the sixth Monday of every month. Generally, we hold luncheon meetings that begin promptly at 9 p.m. I was made the president of our club by acclimation. Nobody showed up to vote against me.

I'm not sure how I got this honor, because we have in our club probably the greatest procrastinator of all time. His twin brother is three years older than he is.

Usually, our meetings are orderly. We begin with an announcement that the minutes of the last meeting will be read at the next meeting. Once, we did have a little flare-up, though. It got so violent that the vice president threw a punch at the treasurer. The treasurer immediately said he would hit him back in about a week or so.

Our next big club event is scheduled for July 4th. It's our annual Christmas party. We expect almost 100 percent nonattendance.

There's one quote by some unknown sage that was omitted from the earlier collection in this chapter because it serves more of a purpose here. It has to do with those of us who have been procrastinating much longer than our younger counterparts. This wise man said, "You know you're getting older when it takes too much effort to procrastinate."

As we grow older, it takes more time and effort to put things off. My advice would be that if you're going to procrastinate, do it now. That's what I did, as this following tale explains:

One day, I decided that America is a great country—home of the free and land of the brave. She is a nation who certainly deserves a great novel. Mark Twain has written some fair ones. Hemingway, Faulkner, Fitzgerald, Jones, Mailer, Capote—they did some OK work, too. *Gone with the Wind* has enjoyed a modicum of success. Still, the great American novel has not been written—until now.

I feel ordained to write it. I'm certainly qualified. American born and raised, I've read most of the current best-selling novels and one or two of the classics. I've attended many writing seminars and I own my own computer.

My novel should have some heft to it, probably about 120,000 words. At 1,000 words a day, with weekends off, the great American novel is only twenty-four weeks away from completed manuscript form.

Certainly, writing the great American novel will bring me fame. I'll be gracious to Oprah, deferential to Bill O'Reilly, and patient with Geraldo, and I'll try desperately to treat Dr. Phil as an equal. It'll make me rich, also, but the fame and wealth are trivial perks more to be endured than savored. What's important is "the work."

What will it be about? I don't know yet, but I believe the inspiration will come from above, as did the holy commission. I must write this epic. I must do it now.

But first . . .

I have pencils to sharpen.

"You've been sharpening pencils for about an hour and a half now," my wife said. "What is it you don't want to write now?"

I said, "I don't *don't* want to write anything, but I'm *compelled* to write the great American novel."

"And even though you have a state-of-the-art computer that has a CD player that shows pictures of the Hindenburg disaster, you still have to sharpen seven dozen pencils before you begin?"

Perhaps my novel will be about a creative genius who manages to produce scintillating work despite the sarcasm of his spouse.

"Yes," I said, "I do. Pointy pencils are the symbol of fine literature. They are inspiration to the scribe. They say that Shakespeare could not even begin a playlet without a mugful of sharpened pencils on his writing desk."

"I don't think pencils were invented when Shakespeare was alive."

"No?"

"No."

"Well, all the more pity," I said. "Think of what he might have produced had he had them. I do have them, and I'm going to avail myself of their motivation."

She said, "Fine. Do you want something to eat, or are you going to sharpen through lunch?"

I tell her, "I can't think of food now. I have the great American novel to write."

But first . . .

"What are you doing now?" my wife asked.

"I'm writing the great American novel."

"With a vacuum cleaner?"

"This is all part and parcel of the process," I explained. "Necessary chores for the one selected to write the great American novel."

"To vacuum the rug?"

"Absolutely. First of all, I can't think imaginatively in a dust-tainted ambience. Second, years from now, tourists will flock here to see the room where the great American novel was born. You and I don't want them to stand behind the red velvet guide ropes and think to themselves, *How could that author be so incredibly ingenious amid so many dust bunnies and cobwebs?*"

My wife said, "I wouldn't want them to think that."

"Nor I," I said. "So please leave me to finish my vacuuming so I can get started on the great American novel."

She left, and I was ready to begin.

But first . . .

"Darling," I yelled to my wife.

"Yes," she hollered back.

"What's your Aunt Gert's husband's name?"

"Philo. Uncle Philo."

"How do you spell it?" I asked.

"P-H-I-L-O. Why do you want to know?"

"Because I hate to misspell a person's name."

"No, I mean why do you suddenly want to know Aunt Gert's husband's name?"

"Oh," I said. "Because I'm making a list of people I want to send autographed copies of my novel to."

My wife came into my office. (Apparently, this confrontation needed to be face to face.) "You're making a list of people you want to send autographed copies of your book to?"

"Yes," I said.

She said, "But you haven't written anything yet."

She just didn't understand. "This book," I said, "is going to take the country by storm. The demands on my time will be unbelievable. If I don't get this done now, I'll never get it done, and it's your relatives who are going to be offended."

She left without another word.

I got back to my list and to the beginning of my great American novel. But first . . .

I gathered up some pens, notepads, a thesaurus, my sunglasses, and a few of my very pointy pencils and ambled through the family room towards the back patio.

"Where are you going now?" my wife asked.

"Outside," I said.

"What for?" she said.

"To work."

She said, "Your sharpened pencils, clean rug, and list of distant relatives are in your office. Why are you going outside?"

"There's inspiration in fresh air," I said. "Do you know who wrote outdoors?"

My wife said, "Gauguin."

I said, "He was an artist, not a writer."

My wife said, "No. He was a writer. He just did that painting stuff so he could keep putting off writing the great Tahitian novel."

"I'll be outside," I said, "working on my novel."

I went out to the back patio to work on the great American novel. But first . . .

I fixed a water sprinkler that had been leaking for some time, I straightened the birdbath because it was listing badly, and then I took a few golf swings, because creative writing is hard work and I needed relaxation.

Then my wife spoiled the mood. "Dinner's ready," she said.

I thought about working through the evening meal, but it wouldn't be fair to my project. Even literary genius requires sustenance, and a novel of the proportions I envisioned would demand my full strength. Nutrition was vital to the work.

I ate, had a cup of coffee, then yawned and said, "I'm going to take a warm bath and get to bed early."

My wife said, "Tomorrow are you going to do some actual writing?"

"Of course I am," I said. "As Hugh Prather once wrote, 'If the desire to write is not accompanied by actual writing, then the desire is not to write.'"

"Hugh Prather wrote that?" my wife asked.

"Yes, he did," I said.

"That's profound. I wonder how many pencils he had to sharpen before he wrote that? How long he vacuumed the carpet? How long his list of relatives was? How many sprinklers and birdbaths . . ."

My wife's mumbling trailed off as I left and headed for my bath and bed. No need for me to remain and be made sport of. I had to get up in the morning and begin work on the great American novel. I was already behind.

So remember, good readers: procrastination is too important to put off until tomorrow.

CHAPTER SIXTEEN

EVALUATE YOUR POTENTIAL

"Confidence is the feeling you sometimes have before
you fully understand the situation." —Anonymous

Our quest for any sort of accomplishment should begin with self-examination. Self-help can do and has done wonders, but few of us expect miracles. Despite the hyperbole, the success books rarely promise us anything that we're not realistically capable of acquiring. They wouldn't promise a 5'3" paunchy middle-ager that with meditation and positive thinking he might become the starting center for the Boston Celtics. Nor would they hold out hope for a seventy-two-year-old grandmother to someday invite her grandchildren to come see her perform in the New York City Ballet.

To be fair to the self-help authors, we must be honest with ourselves in our self-evaluation. We must look in the mirror and say to it, as the wicked queen said in Snow White, "Mirror, mirror on the wall, who is the fairest of them all?" The mirror dutifully answered, "Thou, O Fair Queen, art the fairest of them all." That was fine until one day, the mirror, in a fit of honesty, said, "You, my Queen, are fair, it is true. But Snow White is even fairer than you." Now that was a disastrous revelation to the queen, and the rest, as they say, is a pure fairy tale.

The queen wasn't ready for honesty.

However, we must be. It takes courage to look into a mirror seeking reassurance—especially from a mirror that talks.

One of the first steps in self-improvement is to honestly evaluate what we're capable of. That's a difficult task for those of us who have been around for awhile. Many things we were once capable of we're no longer capable of. If you don't believe me, try jumping the net to congratulate your opponent after winning the Senior Tennis Championship at your local club. Age has a way of diminishing some of our skills.

Some of us older folks may not even want to indulge in self-examination. Many of us may simply surrender and say, "I'm not sure what I can do, but I think I either never could do it or have already done it and lost interest."

Our self-analysis, though, should go beyond the physical. Self-help in general presupposes a degree of intelligence. It assumes that we are all smart people. And we are. Our technical name is *Homo sapiens*, which, in Latin, literally means "wise person." However, as we grow older, our intelligence becomes hidden beneath a patina of dumbness. As smart as we are, we all insist on doing dumb things. We may have to flunk ourselves out of the novitiate stage of self-help.

I'll offer myself as an example, but be an honest reader and assess whether you, too, are guilty of some of these dumb actions.

There are extenuating circumstances for many of my illogical actions. Some are the result of tradition, customs that have been embedded in my subconscious. For instance, I was taught as a young child to always turn the hands of a clock in a clockwise direction. I have never had the courage since to see what would happen—to me, to the clock, to the world—if I reset a clock by going in the opposite direction. Also, the plumbing industry can create the most reliable of valves, levers, washers, and whatever. Most of us will still jiggle the handle after flushing the toilet.

I do other silly things—like walk around a ladder rather than under it, or take another route when a black cat crosses my path—because of superstition.

It was once thought to be unsafe to go into the water within one hour of eating. It's been proven untrue, but I still avoid bathing after eating. It just seems safer, healthier.

Many of the dumb things I do, though, are just plain dumb. Not worthy of a true *Homo sapiens*.

A few examples:

I'll pour myself a glass of ice-cold milk. I like the taste of well-chilled milk. Sometimes, though, the milk is not good. I drink a good portion of it down, and then my hair starts to stand up straight, my mouth puckers, and my toes begin to make a fist. It tastes terrible.

So what do I do? I hand the glass to my wife and say, "Here. See if this tastes sour to you."

Brilliant, huh?

Alexander Graham Bell invented a wonderful device: the telephone. It enables us to speak to people far away. Sometimes, though, I think that I can talk to those same people without using the telephone.

What happens is: The phone rings. I set down whatever I'm doing to go and answer it. It rings again as I cross the room. It rings again before I get there.

I want to receive this call, but I'm afraid that the people placing the phone call will grow impatient and hang up before I can pick up the receiver. So I shout to them, "I'm coming, I'm coming."

Homo sapiens, indeed.

Another great invention is the remote control device. What a fabulous time-saver this can be. We can turn the television set on and off without vacating our easy chair. We can change channels without ever going near the television set. Wonderful.

However, this tiny device can easily be misplaced. So I've instructed my family that, in our house, this instrument is always to be kept on top of the television set. So now, if I want to change channels, I have to get up, cross to the television, grab the remote, change the channel, and return the remote to the top of the television set (where I demanded it always be), then return to my chair. Isn't that a wonderful time-saving device?

I've got to renounce this *Homo sapiens* title.

In today's insecure world, we sometimes have to outsmart those who threaten us. I have a solid front door, so I called a workman to install a peephole there—the kind they have in all the hotels. It's to protect against strangers.

So now that the device is in place, I always check when there's a caller at the front door. I look through the peephole, and if I notice that there are strangers there, what do I do? I open the door to see what they want.

The *Homo sapiens* people should demand the title back from me.

I seriously feel that I no longer deserve this classification. I'm not worthy of it. It trivializes the honor for those who truly deserve it. So I have been researching where and how to officially surrender the nomenclature.

I took out an encyclopedia to see if there was any reference within its pages. As I leafed through it, I realized that I truly had to be declared *non–Homo sapiens*. I was moistening my thumb, then turning the pages with my index finger.

Though I generously offer myself and my experiences as examples of occasional dumbness, I refuse to take the rap alone. I've seen and heard enough examples to know that I'm not the only person who is sometimes intelligence challenged.

Once, I was with a friend and we saw a well-known celebrity. My friend was not as reticent as I. He rushed up to the star and said, "Do you know who you are?" *Homo sapiens* seemed an egregious misnomer at that point.

Another time, my wife accompanied me to a business meeting. As we flew to our destination, I was busy reviewing my notes for the upcoming confab while my spouse conversed with the stranger who sat by the window. I wasn't eavesdropping on the conversation, but I did overhear this snippet:

He asked my wife, "How many children do you have?"

She said, "We have three girls and a boy."

He said, "You have three girls and a what?"

Maybe I'm being too judgmental about this gentleman, but I do think he could have figured that out on his own.

The examples continued even after we arrived at the convention. Each morning at the breakfast counter, we'd be entertained by a delightfully exuberant waitress. We laughed at her tales and anecdotes and even told her that she should write a book about her experiences. We assured her that it would be amusing and that she should prepare a manuscript and send it out for publication.

She said, "Oh, no, I'm not good enough to do that. I'd like someone to read it first before I write it."

One day, as we talked to our monologist/waitress, a customer came in and ordered some coffee to go. She said, "I want two sugars and no cream."

Our waitress said, "Oh, Honey, we don't have cream here."

The customer said, "OK, then. I'll have it without milk."

Our company also had a booth at this convention, and we gave away samples of our product. After the event, I talked to one of our workers and asked, "How many samples did we give away?"

He said, "Do you mean total?"

I said, "No, just give me 80 percent and I'll do the math on my own."

Please don't feel that I'm being "holier than thou" about this. I've been guilty of some pretty dumb statements without any help from others. Once, while traveling, I asked a local resident for directions to a certain restaurant.

He said, "Oh, they tore that place down."

I said, "You mean it's not there anymore?"

Pretty clever, huh?

He tried to either top my dumbness or add some sarcasm. He said, "No, after they tore it down, they hauled it away."

So whatever goal you may seek, be sure you're physically able to handle it and intelligent enough to begin your quest.

CHAPTER SEVENTEEN

RECALL YOUR TRIUMPHS

"No man has a good enough memory to become a successful liar."
—Abraham Lincoln

here are moments in all of our lives when our poise deserts us. Like the best man who agonizes so much over having to deliver the toast at the wedding reception that it destroys the entire party for him. How about when you must give an oral book report to the entire class on a novel you've read but hardly understood? Perhaps your boss informs you that you'll make the presentation to the company that is considering your services for its upcoming sales campaign. Your superior eases your mind by casually saying, "Your performance today could determine whether our firm continues in business or not. But . . . just be yourself." There's also the time when you have to meet your future in-laws for the first time. How that meeting goes determines whether you will say "I do" or they will say "No, you don't." Surely you have your own personal anecdotes about similar moments when your knees shook, your sweat glands became overactive, and your mind became inactive. We've all had them.

One self-help book recommends that you counter these anxiety attacks by recalling instances when you were exalted. The time you told a joke at a company banquet and it got three times the amount of laughter you expected. Remember the time you took first place in the science project in school. Of course, there was the time in seventh grade when you finally worked up the courage to ask the prettiest girl in class if she would go to the movies with you on Saturday afternoon—and she said yes. Those memories swell your head and fill your chest with pride and confidence. Simply remembering them, many self-help volumes suggest, will give you the courage to persevere through other ordeals.

This is wonderfully beneficial and effective advice, but only for those who have a working memory. But "recalling" is a young person's game. I have a daughter named Mabel whom I often call Sally. I have a granddaughter named Sally whom I often call Mabel. And I know both of them very well.

I call my dog so many names that she thinks she's part of a herd. I start with the name of the first dog I owned, then I move on to the name of the second dog I owned, then to the third, and on through the entire litany until I finally get the correct name. In fact, by the time I do get around to calling the dog to "come," she looks around to see if all the others I've called are coming, too. She doesn't want to be trampled in a golden retriever stampede.

Now, my doctor says that this is nothing to worry about. He says that this is not a sign that the mind is failing or that it's a precursor of worse things to come. It's my doctor's professional opinion that all people have memory lapses. "All people," he says, "have memory lapses. Forget about it. Don't fret over it." That's comforting. Yet if I miss an appointment with this same doctor, he charges me for it.

I tell him, "I'm sorry. I forgot I had an appointment today."

He says, "I'm sorry, too, but I have to make a living. I have to charge you for the visit."

I say to him, "You told me not to worry about memory. So I missed an appointment. Big deal."

He says, "I don't remember saying that."

(I wonder if he knows his daughter's, his granddaughter's, and his dog's names.)

I tell the doctor, "You did say it. I distinctly remember you saying it."

He laughs at me. "Ha!" he says. "You, of all people, distinctly remember me saying it? You can't remember anything. You have the recall of a cauliflower. In fact, I think your mind is totally gone and that's a precursor of worse things to come."

Now that sounded familiar to me, but I couldn't recall exactly where I'd heard it before. In any case, I got rid of this doctor . . . I think.

Now, I'm not saying all people my age are memory challenged. I have some friends older than I am who have excellent memories. Their memories are so good they can often recall things that never even happened.

Names are especially elusive after a certain age. I watch the game show *Jeopardy!* faithfully. I know all the answers; I just can't think of them. They'll give the answer: "He was the first president of the United States." I'll say something like, "Oh, I know it. It's . . . uh . . . it's the guy with the wig and the wooden teeth." I just can't summon his name. I have a terrible time remembering names, so I try to avoid meeting people that have them. When I tell this to my wife, she doesn't quite believe me.

My wife said, "Oh, that's just an excuse so that you don't have to go out anywhere or take me anyplace."

"It is not," I said.

She said, "It is."

I said, "It is not. I don't like to go out because I can't remember people's names and I get embarrassed . . . and I embarrass you."

"That's baloney and you know it."

"It's not baloney. If that's not the honest truth, then my name is not . . . uh . . . uh . . ."

"Gene."

I said, "Right. Then my name is not Gene."

I was kidding her with that one; I knew my name was Gene. I couldn't think of her name at the time, but I didn't want to bring that up.

Sometimes, though, not recalling names can destroy an otherwise enjoyable evening. For example: the time my wife and I were watching an old movie on television. My wife commented on one of the performers in the film.

She said, "I don't know who that young actor is, but he's very good."

I said, "Yes, he is quite good. You know who he reminds me of?"

She said, "Who?"

I said, "Oh . . . you know."

"No, I don't know," my wife said.

I said, "Oh, he was very famous. Everybody knows him."

She said, "Then tell me his name."

"I can't think of it," I said. "Oh, this is going to bother me all night now."

My wife said, "Apparently, it'll bother me, too."

I said, "It begins with a 'C'."

"Tom Cruise."

I said, "No, older than that."

She said, "Charlie Chaplin."

"Not that old."

My wife said, "Well, we're zeroing in on it."

"I won't be able to enjoy this movie until I think of that name," I said.

My wife said, "I guess I won't either, then."

I began running through a list of names beginning with "C" to jog my memory. "Carlton . . . Carroll . . . Clark . . ."

My wife jumped at that one. "Clark Gable."

I said, "His last name begins with 'C.'"

She said, "Hopalong Cassidy."

"You're not helping," I said.

She decided to be more helpful. "What movie was he in?"

Now *that* was being helpful. I said, "It was that one we saw a couple of years ago."

"Called . . . ?"

I said, "I forget."

She asked, "What was it about?"

"I forget that, too. But anyway, this actor was in it."

She said, "The one whose name starts with 'C'?"

"Right. Carlisle . . . Christopher . . . Callahan . . . oh, I know he was in this movie."

My wife said, "The one you can't remember?"

I said, "No, this is another one."

She said, "Another one you can't remember, I suppose."

"Yeah. He was in it with that actress."

"Which actress?"

"The actress I used to like."

"Which actress you used to like?"

"Oh, you know."

She said, "No, I don't know."

"She was married to that guy."

"Which guy?"

"You know, the big guy, He got in a fight once with Whatshisname."

"Some other guy."

I said, "Yes, some other guy. They got in a fight."

She said, "Two guys whose names you can't remember got in a fight over an actress whose name you can't remember, but they were all in a movie with a title that you can't remember."

I said, "Now you got it."

My wife said, "You know who we're beginning to sound like?"

I said, "Abbott and Costello."

She said, "How come you can remember Abbott and Costello but you can't remember Whatshisname?"

I said, "Don't get mad at me because I can't remember the guy's name."

She said, "You can't remember anything."

From then on, we watched the movie in silence. Well, not exactly silence. We didn't talk to each other, but I kept muttering to myself. I said, "Carmine . . . Clements . . ." Then out of the blue, it hit me:

"Robert Redford," I shouted.

My wife repeated, "Robert Redford?"

I said "Yeah. That's the guy this actor reminds me of—a young Robert Redford. Don't you think so?"

She said, "No."

I said, "Well that's who he reminds me of—Robert Redford."

We watched the film in silence a little longer. My wife then said, "How do you get a 'C' out of Robert Redford?"

I said, "Would you like some popcorn?"

The point of this tale is that any self-help advice that is predicated on remembering something doesn't help those of us who can't remember anything. But now for the good news. (Notice the good news comes at the end of the chapter so you'll be more likely to remember it.) When you want to reinforce your confidence by recalling past triumphs, you can do that with a faulty memory. You can even do it with total amnesia. You can be motivated by achievements you don't remember having.

I can almost hear you wondering while reading through these pages, *How can I take pride in and draw inspiration from something I've done if I don't even remember ever doing it?* It's simple. You don't have to remember doing something to know that you did it. If you come home from an evening out and discover that the bathroom sink is overflowing and the tile floor is covered with water, do you have to stop and think whether you left the faucet running or not? You see the water cascading down over the countertop, so you know you did it. You may not remember that you did it, but you know you did it.

Now for a practical application. Pick out a spot that's a few yards away from wherever you are at the moment. Now get up from whatever you're doing and go to that spot. Now return to where you were before. There . . . you've proven the concept. You know how to walk.

I can hear your rebellion through the pages again. "What does knowing how to walk have to do with anything?" Well, it shows that you learned how to walk at some time or another.

"So what?" I can hear you asking.

Well, you're walking, but you probably don't remember that moment when you first learned to walk. (I say "first learned to walk" because I had a friend who liked to overindulge, and he would learn—or relearn—how to walk every Monday.) Not being able to remember the instant when you walked doesn't detract from the fact that you learned. It's an achievement that you can use to support the self-esteem you might need today.

Walking is not an easy chore. Oh, sure, it might be today, but it wasn't when you were learning. Watch a toddler trying to graduate from crawling on hands and knees to walking erect. It's a difficult, challenging, daring endeavor for the youngster. They try it and fall on their bottoms. Not once, not twice, but over and over and over again. It's humiliating, it's frustrating, and depending on where and how hard you fall, it can be painful.

But those who endured the embarrassment, the disappointment, and the bumps and bruises of constant failure can be proud that they finally learned to walk. You are one of those.

So even though you may not recall the specific moment when you walked, you can profit from the knowledge that you did. Try to imagine an adult who is learning a new skill persevering through all those setbacks. It's difficult to envision, isn't it?

Adults have trouble learning a new language or playing a new instrument. Listen to the colorful language on any golf course in the nation, and you'll realize that learning a new skill can be frustrating.

But in learning to walk, you became an achiever. Be proud of that. Use it now as you face your future in-laws, as you stand to give that oral book report before the class, as you get ready to make the all-important pitch for your company's business, or as you silently rehearse the toast you have to present at the wedding reception for your best friend. (For those of you who don't remember, those are the examples we used in the beginning of this chapter.)

Stand now proudly and self-assuredly. You are an achiever. You've conquered difficulties in the past, whether you remember them or not. You're about to do it again. Bravo, oh you of faulty recall.

Don't fret about what you can't remember. As they say today, "Forget about it." Just stand tall and do a great job. Maybe this one you will remember.

CHAPTER EIGHTEEN

LIVE IN THE PRESENT

"Learn from yesterday, live for today, look to tomorrow, rest this afternoon." —Charles Schulz

H ere's another thing that confuses our aging minds: self-help literature advises us to know exactly what we want and to plan for it. The authors want us to visualize our goals. They suggest that we make plans—immediate plans, short-term plans, long-term plans, plans to use when our original plans don't seem to be working. They recommend that we not only plan but that we prioritize our plans. In other words, we have to plan which plan that we've planned that we should plan on executing before we plan on executing the other plans. All of this is affecting our future.

But we also should study our predecessors. As Isaac Newton humbly said, we stand "on the shoulders of giants." We should learn from the successes of others. We should also benefit from the failures of others. Much of the literature quotes Edison—who reportedly tried over 10,000 different materials before he discovered the one that would work in his lightbulb—something to the effect of "I have not failed. I've just found 10,000 ways that won't work."

The authors recommend that we recall our own achievements and use them as inspiration for further accomplishments. All of this is utilizing the past.

So we're bombarded with admonitions about the past and proposals for the future. Then they blindside us with "Always try to live in the present moment."

We're supposed to focus on the past and plan for the future, all while thinking about nothing but the present moment. It's confounding for our aging minds. It's oxymoronic. It's like trying to jump across a well in two jumps.

Should we focus on the past, the present, or the future? Most of them recommend living in the present moment, but there really is no such thing as the present moment. It doesn't really exist. As soon as we concentrate on this present moment, it disappears into the past. The present moment, in a fraction of a nanosecond, becomes the moment that just passed. And the present moment, which we're trying to live in right now, was the future just a nanosecond ago. Then that future turned to the present, and before we realized it was the present, it became the past. Are you keeping up with all of this?

In a strange, ironic way, though, it makes sense. Reliving the past is a waste of time. It's done. It's finished. It's written in indelible ink. Think about the past all you want, but you won't change a moment of it. It's impossible.

The one good thing about thinking of past events is that you can always be right. Monday-morning quarterbacks always make the right choice because they know the catastrophic results of making the wrong choice. Some people have gained notoriety as psychics and prophets. They can predict the future. However, we're all psychics and prophets when it comes to past events. We can all accurately predict events that have already happened.

So if you want to be right all the time, focus on the past. It's like taking an open-book exam. You can't fail.

The future is trickier. The past has happened, so you should know what happened. The future hasn't happened yet, so we're all only guessing. Even if you are a true prognosticator and can boast 100 percent accuracy, it does you no good. You're predicting things that have not yet happened. Listeners won't know that you're correct until those things in the future actually do occur. And once they do occur, they become events of the past. Everyone now knows they happened, so why do they need you to tell us they were going to happen? Are you still keeping up with all of this?

To review, the past is gone. You can do nothing about it. The future is merely a guess. Your guess may be right, but you won't know that until it happens, and as soon as it happens, it becomes the past. So all you have is the present moment. Take advantage of it. But take advantage of it quickly, because—*whoosh*— there it goes. It's now the past.

Considering that the earth is roughly 4.58 billion years old, not having to think about that—the past—is a tremendous load off our minds. Assuming that we're going to continue for at least that long into the future, and there are no indications so far to the contrary, that's another 4.58 billion years that we needn't be concerned with. That's at least 9.16 billion years that we can ignore while we focus only on that fraction of a fraction of a fraction of a second that is the present moment. It seems simple, doesn't it? Yet we often fail even at that mundane task.

Consider this tale:

My wife and I travel many places together. Wherever we're going, we usually take one car because it's cheaper and it's one less parking space to look for. We listen to pleasant music that we both enjoy or we talk to one another, converse, communicate. Usually, that is.

This time, though, we drove in silence. We didn't have to. We could have had a conversation like this:

I say, "How long did you go out with that guy in high school? What was his name? Weasel or Muskrat or something?"

She says, "His name was Moose. And we didn't go out together. We just dated a lot."

"How long?"

She says, "One year, four months, two weeks, three days, and twelve hours."

"But you weren't going out together?" I ask.

"We just dated," she says.

"Ox played football, didn't he?"

"Moose. His name was Moose. And I'll say he played football. He still holds the league record for yards gained."

"What? A couple hundred yards?"

My wife is offended at this miniscule guess. She says, "His career record is 3,716 yards."

"That's a lot, huh?"

She says, "He averaged 4.6 yards per carry over a three-year career."

I'm impressed. "Three years!"

"That's right. He started in thirty-seven games, which is still a school record, and ran for 100 yards or more in fourteen separate games."

I say, "You certainly know a lot about Whale."

"His name is Moose. And yes, I know everyone of his football statistics by heart."

I say, "I didn't think you liked football that much."

She says, "I didn't. I liked Moose."

"I understand," I say, and we let the conversation rest for awhile.

Later I ask, "Do you remember that girl, Sally?"

She asks, "Which girl Sally?"

"The one we met at my nephew Charlie's wedding?"

She asks, "She was sitting with your cousin Billy, right?"

"That's the one."

She says, "Yes, I remember her."

I say, "How do I know her?"

She says, "You're related to her."

"Well, I know that," I say. "But how?"

"She's your cousin."

"But how?" I ask.

She says, "She's John's Sally."

I say, "John who?"

"Your Uncle John."

I say, "I didn't know I had an Uncle John."

My wife explains, "Well, you don't really. He's your Uncle Phil's brother."

"Who's Uncle Phil?"

"Uncle Phil is married to your father's sister, Harriet. Uncle John is Phil's brother, so, technically, he's not your uncle."

"So he's not my Uncle John."

"That's what I just said," she says.

"Then how is Sally my cousin?"

"Because John used to be your uncle."

"Then what? He flunked the physical?"

"No," my wife says, getting impatient with my ignorance. "Uncle John used to be married to your father's other sister, Sarah."

"Yeah?" I want her to go on.

"Sally is their daughter, so she's your cousin. But John divorced your Aunt Sarah and married his present wife, Myrtle."

"She's not related to me."

"No."

"Then Uncle John's not my uncle and Aunt Myrtle's not my aunt."

"That's true, but out of courtesy, you call them 'Aunt' and 'Uncle.'"

I say, "I don't even know them."

"But the rest of the family calls them Uncle John and Aunt Myrtle."

I clarify, "But they're not my aunt and uncle."

"Technically, no."

"So, how is Sally my cousin?"

My wife patiently (well, not so patiently) explains, "Because Sally was born when John was married to your father's sister, your Aunt Sarah."

I say, "So technically she remains my cousin, but also technically Uncle John is no longer my uncle and Aunt Myrtle is completely unrelated to me."

My wife says, "Now you've got it."

I say, "I don't even know what I'm talking about."

She says, "Well, you've got it right anyway."

I say, "Boy, you know more about my family than I do."

She says, "I know more about everything than you do."

We give the conversation another rest.

Later I ask, "Did our kids have the measles?"

My wife says, "Sure, Christopher had them in July of '76, and the girls had the measles one right after the other. That was in August and September of '79."

"How about chicken pox?" I ask.

My wife says, "Christopher and Patricia had it in November of '80. Sheila never had it."

We're silent for a short while, and then I ask, "Can you name Santa's reindeer?"

She says, "Certainly. I used to read that poem to the children all the time." She quotes, "Now Dasher, now Dancer, now Prancer, now Vixen. On Comet, on Cupid, on Donner and Blitzen. And then there's Rudolph, of course."

I ask, "Can you name the seven dwarfs?"

"Sure. You got your Dopey, Sleepy, Sneezy, Happy, Grumpy, Doc, and Bashful."

I say, "That's good. Now can you name the Four Horsemen?"

"Who are the Four Horsemen?"

"They're famous football players. I thought maybe you and Ox talked about them in high school."

"His name is Moose, and you know it. What's this all about, anyway?"

I say, "Well, I was just wondering. You can remember all of Moose's records, how everyone in my family is related, when the kids had different diseases, Santa's reindeer, and the seven dwarfs."

"Yeah, so?"

"So, if you can remember all that junk from the past, why are we driving back to the house to see if you remembered to unplug the curling iron in the upstairs bathroom?"

We might have had that conversation, but we didn't. We just drove toward the house in grim silence.

CHAPTER NINETEEN

OVERCOMING FEAR

"Courage can overcome fear ... almost as well as
hiding under the bed." —Anonymous

Sir Francis Bacon said it originally, but Franklin Delano Roosevelt immortalized the quote in his first inaugural speech. He said, "We have nothing to fear but fear itself." Probably William Shakespeare said it most eloquently in his play *Measure for Measure*:

Our doubts are traitors
And make us lose the good we oft might win
By fearing to attempt.

Most self-help authors suggest that fear is the enemy of achievement. Being afraid can hamper us so much that we fail to deliver our maximum effort. In other words, we might have won if we hadn't been so afraid of losing. Fear can also prompt us to give up without even competing. We're so afraid that we might not win that we don't even try. As Shakespeare wisely noted, we "lose the good we oft might win by fearing to attempt."

None of us are strangers to fear, though. So the self-help advocates skirt that reality by claiming that courage is not the absence of fear but rather the mastery of it. Someone once defined courage as the ability to not let anyone else know that you're afraid. Some wise self-help author even advised that, under all circumstances, be brave. Even if you're not, pretend, because no one can tell the difference.

Sometimes you can have a fear of something and courageously deny it. Woody Allen used to say that he was not afraid of death—he just didn't want to be there when it happened.

Fear is particularly troublesome because it is so ubiquitous. There are so many different types of terror. Name almost anything, and someone will have an inordinate fear of it. Here are a few:

- Pteridophobia: That's a fear of ferns. It's a fear of normal, harmless ferns. (Of course, we all have a fear of the dreaded man-eating ferns.)
- Leukophobia: This is a fear of the color white. If you have this one, forget about working in a hospital or becoming a Good Humor man.
- Bibliophobia: This is a fear of books. Probably no one currently reading this book has this fear.
- Triskaidekaphobia: This is the common fear of the number thirteen. I wonder, though, if people who fear thirteen also have a fear of seventeen minus four?
- Trypophobia: This is a fear of holes. Once, they had a convention of these folks, and it was disastrous. They made the mistake of serving Swiss cheese sandwiches at the luncheon.
- Pittakionophobia: Get this, it's the fear of stickers—the common, ordinary paste-on kind. Strangely enough, this is a new term for it. It used to be called "panniophobia." That was probably in the old days when people used to have a fear of words with too many syllables in them. Who knows?

- Lophobia: You'll love this one—it's a fear of dust bunnies. If you know anyone who has this phobia, don't ever let them look under your bed.
- I think they should also have one called "phobiaphobia." That would be a fear of being afraid of something.

Admittedly, these are weird fears, and you may suffer from them and not even know it. For instance, you could be a victim of lutraphobia, which is a fear of otters. I was born and raised in a city, so I'm not afraid of otters, because I've never seen an otter. However, if I ever did see one, I might be paralyzed with terror. Who knows? Probably the otter would sense it and would attack me immediately. So, you see, I would have good reason to be afraid.

That's the insidious thing about fear—you can have it and not even know you have it. I never thought I suffered from arachnophobia. I'm not fond of spiders. They're not particularly affectionate critters, but I wasn't scared of them . . . until this one day as I walked to my car that was parked in the driveway. A giant spider was smack in my path. Simply the immensity of it startled me. When I first saw it, it looked like a Volkswagen with legs where the wheels should be. It was larger than the room I lived in during my college days.

The creature measured a full five inches from the tip of its whatever-is-at-the-front-most-part-of-a-spider to the bottom of its whatever-is-at-the-hindmost-part-of-a-spider. To my generation, that's considered "huge"; to the younger generation, that's considered "humongous."

I don't know much about spiders, but if they do have faces, this one had a mean look on his or her face. If spiders don't have faces, this one had a sinister snarl on whatever they use in place of a face.

My first thought was to tiptoe around it without disturbing it or provoking a skirmish. It didn't look like it would cooperate with that strategy. I was faced with a fight-or-flight decision. If I chose flight, where would I run to? If I chose fight, I would obviously be conquered and devoured, and I was already late for work. So I did what most people would do in a similar situation. I assumed a pose that implied that I was trained in karate. Of course, this was dumb. How many spiders go to Jean-Claude Van Damme movies?

So I stared at the critter, and it stared back at me. Neither one of us would advance, and neither one of us would yield. I could almost hear this spider's tiny little brain saying silently, *C'mon, man, make my day.* (Apparently, spiders don't go to Jean-Claude Van Damme movies but they do go to Clint Eastwood flicks.)

Just then, my wife came out of the front door and said, "Haven't you left yet? You're going to be late for work."

I said, "That giant spider is keeping me from reaching the car."

She went over to it, stamped her foot on the ground, and said, "Shoo."

The frightened spider scurried away to the safety of the bushes that framed our driveway. My wife turned and walked calmly back into the house.

So that's one way I learned to overcome fear—have your wife handle it.

Of course, the self-help authors don't write too much about fear of otters or spiders or the color white or the number thirteen. However, they do harp on the fear of failure. Again, refer back to William Shakespeare's admonition: "Our doubts are traitors and make us lose the good we oft might win by fearing to attempt."

But we older folks don't seem to fear failure. You see, fear seems to melt away the more times you confront it. In fact, repeated bouts with fear can generate courage. You just get so used to being afraid that your attitude resembles bravery. And we older citizens have faced fear time and time again. We've had to—it's the only way to get this far along in life. Some of us have endured so much fear that now we appear valiant. We're not. We just no longer give a damn.

There's one fear that defies this strategy, though. It's a monumental fear that can hamper our quest for success. Hardly any offensive can conquer it. It's the fear of public speaking. In fact, a survey taken by somebody somewhere listed "speaking in public" as the number one fear of people.

Folks fear public speaking more than anything. More than being attacked by a giant squid. More than getting your lower lip caught under a manhole cover. More than *anything*. The fear of public speaking was ranked higher than the fear of death. That means that at a funeral, more people would rather be in the casket than have to stand at the lectern and deliver the eulogy.

I've tried to conquer this fear by confronting it. I agreed to speak to a roomful of people. I learned two things from that experience: I learned that I had hands, and I learned that I had no idea what I should do with them.

I furtively looked at my hands hanging down at my side and said to myself, *Why did I bother to bring these?*

They felt to me like tonsils or an appendix. They probably serve some useful purpose on the human body, but at this particular moment, I couldn't figure out what that might be.

I hadn't even begun to speak yet, but I was panicking. I knew that everyone in the auditorium was staring at my hands—including me. I think people who weren't even supposed to be at this talk poked their heads in the door just to take a look at my hands.

I had never really noticed these appendages before. I had taken them for granted. Now, I studied them. I learned, for instance, that my hands were approximately twelve times the size of my head. That's right—they were huge. And they weighed eighty-four pounds each.

I forgot about my notes and my audience and concentrated only on those hands. They grew larger and heavier, and they seemed to get further and further from my shoulders. That's right. They were actually growing closer to the floor.

They were an embarrassment, and I had no idea what to do with them. They no longer fit into my pockets. Then I thought, *Hey, why not use them for gesturing?* Great idea.

So I decided to begin my speech (I hadn't said a word yet) with a sweeping motion of my right hand. It wouldn't move. It just hung there. I thought maybe I'd make the dramatic sweeping motion with my left hand instead (a good speaker should always be ambidextrous). The other hand wouldn't move, either.

These were my hands. They were dangling from my shoulders, but someone must be operating them with a remote control device. I certainly had no influence over them. I did notice that when I turned my shoulder slightly, they swayed. If I turned my shoulders more, they swayed harder and farther. So I did that for awhile. The audience checked their programs. Was this a speaker or a puppet show?

I had to say something, so I said, "Uhhhhmmmmm," and I kept saying that for about a minute. Someone towards the back of the room yelled, "We can't hear you." The microphone was too low to pick up my voice.

I panicked even more. How could I adjust the microphone? I couldn't use my hands. I couldn't lift them. They now weighed 104 pounds each. That's right. They had gained twenty pounds apiece in that short time. So I bent at the knees and at the waist and spoke directly into the microphone.

Beginning again, I repeated "Uhhhhmmmmm" for those who hadn't heard it the first time. In my Groucho Marx–like stance, with my knuckles scraping the floor, I continued my speech.

It failed miserably. The opening "Uhhhmmmmm" was the highlight of my presentation. Since this speech was to a group of recovering senior citizens at a convalescent home, I thought I had an appropriate finish, at least; I said to them, "Goodbye, and I hope you all get better soon."

A lady sitting in the front row said, "We hope you do, too."

So despite what the self-help writers say, I've surrendered to my fears. I stay far away from otters. I avoid confrontations with spiders. I steer clear of dust bunnies, too. If I play ball on the old-timers' softball team, I refuse to wear the number thirteen jersey. You won't catch me anywhere near a podium or a lectern or a microphone. And I'm done with speaking in public. I definitely will "lose the good I oft might win by fearing to attempt." I advise you follow my example. If the senior citizens' convalescent home ever calls and asks you to give a speech, tell them to contact William Shakespeare. He oft might do it.

CHAPTER TWENTY

SELF-ESTEEM

"Those people who think they know everything are a great annoyance to those of us who do." —Isaac Asimov

Perhaps legitimate self-esteem is best defined by an example:

A barroom in a small western town was crowded with rowdy cowhands washing trail dust away with cheap whiskey and playing noisy games of poker. Suddenly, the swinging doors burst open and a tall, ominous stranger stepped into the saloon. He shouted in a loud, gruff voice, "I'm Black Bart, and I want every low-down, sidewinding, lily-livered, yellow-bellied, sniveling, son-of-a-polecat coward to get out of here . . . right now!"

Boots shuffled, chairs scraped along the rough floor, tables were turned over, poker chips were scattered, bar girls screamed, and everyone rushed to scamper past the fierce intruder and out the swinging doors. Everyone except for one cowpoke, who calmly sat finishing his drink.

The treacherous interloper marched directly to the seated cowboy and repeated in a louder and even gruffer tone, "I'm Black Bart, and I said I want every low-down, sidewinding, lily-livered, yellow-bellied, sniveling, son-of-a-polecat coward to get out of here . . . right now!"

The cowboy calmly looked up at the tall stranger and said, "There sure were a lot of them, weren't there?"

That's self-esteem.

Self-esteem is thinking highly of yourself. Often, it's thinking highly of yourself despite compelling evidence to the contrary. You must tell yourself, for example, "I am the greatest figure skater in the world." If you are the greatest figure skater in the world, that statement is relatively easy to make. If you're not the greatest figure skater in the world, it's a bit of a fib. But the better you can fib to yourself, the greater your self-esteem should be.

Humility, on the other hand, is thinking highly of yourself but hiding it from others. You say to your associates "I'm not a very good figure skater" while secretly repeating to yourself "I'm the greatest figure skater on earth." One of the above statements has got to be a fib. Conceivably, both of them are.

So right off the bat, self-esteem is rife with duplicity.

Deception also factors into self-esteem by using inaccurate statements as a cover for poor performance. To stick with our previous example, you admit that you may not be the greatest figure skater in the world, but (here comes the subterfuge) you claim that "it's not my fault." Perhaps it's because your parents couldn't afford to pay for the necessary lessons. Perhaps the reason is that you lived in the wrong part of the country. Maybe you were forced to spend an inordinate amount of time studying useless subjects instead of practicing your leaps and turns. Maybe you had early injuries that hampered your development. Maybe your instructors favored other students over you. Maybe there was a concerted effort among the future figure skaters of the world to unfairly discredit you. Whatever the reason, you could have been the greatest figure skater in the world except for that.

It works nicely, doesn't it?

Let me give you another more personal example. I was playing a doubles tennis match with some friends. I am probably the greatest tennis player in the world. At one particular point during this match, we volleyed back and forth several times with neither team establishing an advantage. Then the opponent threw up a lob. It was an easy shot for me, the greatest tennis player in the world. All I had to do was take aim, take my time, and viciously slam the ball into the opposing court for an outright win. Instead, I whiffed. I, the self-declared greatest tennis player in the world, missed the ball completely. It was embarrassing.

Rather, it *could* have been embarrassing had I not had an appropriate excuse.

I explained to my playing partner, "The sun was in my eyes." Not even the greatest tennis player in the world can effectively hit an overhead smash when blinded by the sun. Never mind the fact that we were playing this match on an indoor tennis court. Meaning that we, the players, were indoors while the sun was outdoors. I still insisted that the sun was in my eyes. If not, I would have hit a decisive, winning return.

I maintained my tennis self-esteem.

Many self-help authors bluntly state that self-esteem is the single most important factor on the road to success. Believing you can do it, believing you deserve it, and believing you can get it are the essential elements in eventually getting "it."

Norman Vincent Peale has been quoted as saying, "People become really quite remarkable when they start thinking that they can do things. When they believe in themselves, they have the first secret of success."

An old French proverb tells us, "One is rated by others as he rates himself."

So the experts seem to agree that effective self-esteem is the starting point of any worthwhile quest . . . or it should be, anyway. Most of the authors imply that trying to accomplish anything without self-esteem is like doing the breaststroke in a swimming pool full of cake batter.

A setback for us older self-improvers is that developing workable self-esteem becomes more and more difficult the longer you work at it. It is based on a series of *little white lies*, and those get less and less white as the years go by. As youngsters, we may even believe a few of them. Some of them actually work, and we may achieve the goals we sought. But as we get into our advancing years, we tend to notice that many of the things we told ourselves about ourselves have not been true. We can still tell our little white fibs if we choose, but we become more skeptical of our own pronouncements.

Nevertheless, we try to trick ourselves—and as many others as we can—into thinking that we're better than we actually are. There are times when it's difficult to pull off this hoax. Another reality is that sometimes our self-trickery can backfire on us. That can be painful. The following tale illustrates this:

My wife and I were planning an excursion. We both graduated from the same grade school in the same year, and we were going to drive cross country to attend a reunion of that graduating class. These were people we had known from kindergarten through eighth grade, most of whom we hadn't seen since. It was an event well worth traveling from the West Coast to the East Coast to attend.

We shared chores in preparation. My wife cleaned the vehicle and stocked it. She also did the research, marked the road maps, and made calls to reserve space for our stops along the way. I went out and bought a $1,200 suit.

"What did you buy a $1,200 suit for?" my wife asked.

I said, "Look, we haven't seen a lot of these folks since we got out of grade school. I want to look great for them."

"You can look great in your old suit."

"No," I said. "I want to look like I'm doing better than anybody else there."

"We were probably doing better than some of them until you spent $1,200 for a suit."

"This suit is meant to build my self-esteem."

"We can't afford $1,200 for a suit."

"You know that, and I know that, but they don't know that."

"The store will know it at the end of the month when the bill comes due."

"I'll manage somehow," I said.

"I hope they change the location of the reunion to Phoenix."

"Why?"

"Because that's about as far as we're going to get since you spent our gas money on a new suit."

We got to our reunion on the East Coast without running out of gas money. The first event on the agenda was a church service, so the greetings of many old friends were subdued. Out of reverence, we just smiled at each other and nodded. For extra special old friends, we'd open our eyes real wide and wave cutely.

When I attended this school, I was selective about my friends. My parents, of course, warned me about the dangers of getting in with the wrong crowd. I was careful.

I was even more careful at this gathering. I glanced around the crowd during the church service to seek out people I could be chummy with during the dinner and the party. In particular, I was looking for people whose suits didn't look as expensive as mine.

In my school days, I didn't like some of these kids. They had a bad attitude, which meant they either had a better bike than I did, they lived in a bigger house than I did, or their parents made more money than mine did—bad attitudes like that. This particular evening, I didn't like many of them because they had hair. Those I *definitely* didn't want sitting at my table during dinner.

I searched frantically, trying to find, before this church service concluded, someone who looked not as well-to-do as I and my $1,200 suit looked. More important, I wanted someone who looked older than I was. It was tough. As the end of the service drew nearer, I relaxed my demands. Now I searched for someone who appeared as old as I did. It was still tough.

Finally, I honed in on my target. I had no idea who he was. I didn't remember him as a classmate. Of course, he could have changed dramatically since his elementary school days. Obviously, he wouldn't have been bald then. He was now. He probably didn't have that paunch back in the seventh and eighth grades. He had one now. He didn't wear a $1,200 suit when he graduated, but he had one now. I could forgive him for that, though, since he had so many other wonderful qualities that nominated him as my evening's buddy.

When the church service ended, we all gathered outside and the squeals of recognition, handshaking, backslapping, and tearful hugging began in earnest. I said a few sedate "Hello"s to acquaintances I recognized or who recognized me, but I didn't linger in small talk. I was stalking my prey. I wanted to get close to the guy who looked heavier, balder, and older than me—even though he wore a suit of comparable price.

I spotted him with a group and joined into their conversation. An old girlfriend from those days opened her eyes wide when she saw me, rushed over, and gave me a huge hug and a sincere kiss. We exchanged "How are you doing"s and "What are you up to"s before things settled back to what they were before I joined them.

My former girlfriend then grabbed the hand of the man I had targeted. The fatter, balder, older guy I had intended to stand next to for the entire evening. She pulled him towards me and said, "You remember my dad, don't you?"

A small fortune spent on a self-esteem-boosting suit shot to hell.

Maybe we all should simply be honest about who and what we are and be happy about it. That could be the real self-esteem.

CHAPTER TWENTY-ONE

LEARN FROM OTHERS

"We are all here on earth to help others; what on earth the others are here for, I don't know." — John Foster Hall

Some comedian once said, "A bachelor is a man who never makes the same mistake once." Another wise man commented on mistakes, saying, "No one ever makes the same mistake twice. The first time you make it, it's a mistake. Anytime after that, it's a choice."

The late comedian Henny Youngman had a joke in his act: "I said, 'Doctor, it hurts when I do this.' The doctor said, 'Then don't do that.'" It's a funny gag, and it's also very simple, logical advice.

One gentleman was a rookie factory worker who foolishly put his fingers too close to some whirling piece of machinery. There was a gruesome mechanical sound—*Bbbrrrrppppfff*—and the poor victim yelled in pain. Another worker rushed over and asked, "What happened?"

The rookie worker said, "I put my finger in there, and . . ." Again there was that sound of machinery gone horribly awry—*Bbbrrrrppppfff*—and the worker screamed again and then said, "How about that? It did it again."

We all make mistakes, of course, but smart people learn from them. We learn not to do that again. The even smarter people learn from the mistakes of others. Like the comedian's bachelor, we learn not to make the same mistake once. Let others make the mistake. Let them suffer the consequences. The alternative, of course, would be to make all the mistakes yourself, but that would be time consuming.

There is no shortage of mistakes in the world. Mistakes are out there in abundance, and you're welcome to learn from them. It's like getting a free education. No one charges you to see their mistakes. In fact, if you make a mistake, everyone will know about it almost immediately.

If you go to a black tie event and you wear an impeccable tuxedo, no one notices that. It's not a mistake. But show up with one black sock and one red one, and everyone in the ballroom will know about it. And they will learn from that. They'll make a mental note: *Don't show up to a black tie affair wearing two different-colored socks. And if you do, make sure one of them isn't red.*

But isn't it better to see someone else make that error and learn from it?

Observe people who do what you aspire to do. Find out what mistakes they make now or what mistakes they have made along the way. Then, as Henny Youngman's doctor advised, don't do that.

Another way to learn from other people's mistakes is to hang around with a bunch of folks who tend to do things incorrectly. You'll have an abundance of blunders you can learn to avoid. It can be quite educational. Granted, you'll be spending a good deal of time with a bunch of losers, but it's for a good cause.

You can also generate errors from others that you can benefit from. Goad your friends into making mistakes.

"Hey Charlie, you know what you should do?"

"What?" Charlie dutifully asked.

"You should go over and run with the bulls in Pamplona."

"What? Are you crazy? That's dangerous."

"No," I said. "It's fun."

"Those bulls are big, man."

"Yes, they are big, but they use trick bulls."

"Trick bulls?"

I said, "Yeah. A lot of people don't know about that."

"You really think it'll be fun?"

I said, "Sure. It's an adventure. When you come back, you'll be a hero."

"You're sure they use trick bulls?"

"Absolutely," I said.

So Charlie booked a flight to Spain and ran with the bulls through the streets of Pamplona. Apparently, this particular year they were low on trick bulls, so they had to use the regular kind. Charlie came back on crutches, with his right arm in a sling, and with several cuts and bruises in sundry places.

But I learned from Charlie's mistake. I learned it's not safe to run with the bulls in Pamplona. I also learned never to trust supposed friends who tell you "they use trick bulls."

I go out of my way to help those I love learn from other people's mistakes. Many times, those mistakes they benefit from are mine. This incident with my granddaughter comes to mind:

"Pop-Pop, why do things break?"

That question from my three-year-old granddaughter was the only cloud in an otherwise pleasant, sunny, perfect summer day. It was a morning that was ideal for teeing up the Titleist on the first hole at South Valley Country Club, exchanging insults with my partners, debating whether this putt is a "gimme" or should be holed out, and recounting good and bad shots over lunch in the men's lounge. That's what I thought it was ideal for. My wife decided it was a suitable day for fixing several of the recalcitrant sprinkler heads in our back lawn. So we compromised, as we'd done throughout our long marriage: I fixed the sprinkler heads in our back lawn.

I'm not good at handyman projects. I once bought a hammer and had to take it back to the store because it didn't come with instructions. I have a toolbox that my wife keeps locked away with the keys hidden in a secure place. I just am not gifted with tools. Yet my wife decided that I should attempt to fix the sprinklers. She felt it was a relatively simple project that a child—or even I—could do.

But whenever I begin a do-it-yourself project, I never do-it-myself. I always have someone help me. If nothing else, it's someone to blame. I recall once when I was first married, I had my new bride help me with some home repairs. I was fouling them up, but I tried to blame it on my helper. In a weak moment, I said something to my spouse that I shouldn't have said, wished I hadn't said, wished I could have grabbed the words out of midair and pulled them back and out of existence. But you can't do that.

I said to my spouse, "I don't understand how someone like you can be so incredibly beautiful and at the same time so incredibly dumb."

Thankfully, she kept her sense of humor. She said, "I think God made me incredibly beautiful so you'd be attracted to me. And I think he made me incredibly dumb so I'd be attracted to you."

This day, I had my granddaughter helping me. Again, I knew with tools in my hand, I would make some flagrant mistakes. This was an opportunity for her to learn from other people's mistakes—in this case, her Pop-Pop.

I answered her question about why things break by telling her, "Things break when they get old."

She said, "Are you going to break?"

I said, "I came very close to breaking this morning when Mom-Mom wanted me to skip golf and fix the sprinklers." That's the nice thing about answering questions for a three-year-old—even if they don't understand the reply, they accept it anyway. But they always have another question.

"Why are you fixing them now?" she wanted to know.

I said, "For two reasons." I struggled to loosen the damaged sprinkler head, which didn't want to be loosened. "First, because this thing is broken now. Second, because your Mom-Mom said I should fix it . . . now."

"My mommy says I should always do what she says. Do you always have to do what Mom-Mom says?"

I said, "Yes, dear. Pop-Pops learn very early to do whatever Mom-Moms say."

"Why?"

I evaded that question while banging on the sprinkler head that refused to be unseated. "Well, Honey, I'd answer that question for you, but by the time I finished, you'd be a Mom-Mom yourself and you would already know the answer."

Perceptively, she asked, "Is Mom-Mom your boss?"

Although I was struggling with this reluctant sprinkler head, I said, "No, Honey. Mom-Mom decides the little things—what we're having for dinner, when the sprinklers need fixing, and things like that. Pop-Pop makes all the big decisions."

"Like what?"

"Well, we've only been married forty-six years, so we haven't had one yet."

She looked puzzled at that reply, but it didn't stop her from asking another question: "Pop-Pop, why did you throw that thing into the bushes?"

I said, "That thing is a wrench, and it's supposed to get this thing off of that thing, but it's not doing it, so Pop-Pop threw it into the bushes because Pop-Pop never wants to see it again."

"Why?"

"Because Pop-Pop doesn't need it anymore. Pop-Pop's going to use this thing to fix this dad-burned sprinkler head." I showed her my hammer, and I didn't exactly use the word "dad-burned." I used some other words.

"My mommy says I shouldn't use words like that," she told me.

I said, "Your mommy's right, but your mommy's out shopping with your Mom-Mom, and your Pop-Pop is here fixing the dad-burned sprinklers." (This time, I did use the word "dad-burned.")

She asked, "What does 'dad-burned' mean?"

I said, "It means the same as those other words Pop-Pop used before, only not as well."

She puzzled over that reply while I took a hearty swing at the uncooperative sprinkler head. That released the sprinkler head by breaking it off completely. Water shot high into the air, all over me and my granddaughter.

"Oh, that was fun, Pop-Pop! Can you do it again?"

"Sure I can, Honey. Watch this." And I took a swipe at another sprinkler head that wasn't even broken—until now. We had another fountain of water to enjoy.

"This is fun, Pop-Pop!" she shouted as she ran back and forth under the fallout from the geysers.

I joined her, getting soaked. I said, "If you think this is fun, wait 'til you see what happens when Mom-Mom gets home."

When Mom-Mom did get home, she found a sopping wet backyard, a sopping wet husband, and a sopping wet granddaughter. The sopping wet backyard just laid there, but the sopping wet spouse and granddaughter were having a wonderful time laughing, rolling in mud, and enjoying the day that was perfect for golf, for sprinkler repairs, and, obviously, for playing with grandchildren.

The little one ran to her mother and said, "Mommy, Pop-Pop and I had fun playing in the yard. And I learned why things break."

Her mom asked, "Why do things break?"

She said, "They break when Pop-Pop tries to fix them."

She was right. She had learned from my mistakes.

Mom-Mom learned from my mistakes, too. She learned to go inside and call the sprinkler repairman.

CHAPTER TWENTY-TWO

NO MAN IS AN ISLAND

"A conference is a gathering of important people who singly can do nothing but together can decide that nothing can be done."
—Fred Allen

Self-help advocates preach that "no man is an island." This has nothing to do with people being surrounded by a body of water (although for some people, that's not a bad idea). It implies that we are all connected in one way or another to each other and that we must work with one another in order to succeed. We can't do it alone.

That's a demoralizing concept. Every person I've ever known, currently know, or will come to know has at least one characteristic that is irritating. At least, to me it's irritating. In fact, that's one reason why we older folks are not that eager to get to know people too well. The better we know them and they know us, the more likely it is that we'll uncover that particular trait that irritates us.

Some days, I'll come home from the golf club and complain to my wife, "Boy, I had to play eighteen holes with Griswald today. I hate to play with Griswald."

My spouse is an understanding, forgiving, and reasonable person. She'll usually reply, "Well maybe Griswald doesn't enjoy playing with you either." She's right, which incidentally is one characteristic of my wife that I find annoying.

I try to dissuade her with logic. I say, "Just because I don't enjoy playing golf with Griswald is no excuse for his not enjoying playing golf with me. Griswald is annoying; I'm charming."

My wife just smirks, which is another of her characteristics that I find irritating.

I'm not exempting myself from this irritation factor. I'm as guilty as the next man. I don't know how many idiosyncrasies I have that annoy various people, but I do know of one that irritates almost everyone. I'm a hummer. Most of the time I don't know I'm doing it, but most of the time I'm doing it. I hum constantly and anywhere.

I'm an usher at church services on Sunday. I hum as I take up the collection. It would be acceptable if I hummed religious music. Collecting donations while humming "Amazing Grace" would be appropriate. But no. I hum tunes like the "Beer Barrel Polka." It's difficult to make that sound sacred.

I've had churchgoers who have said, "Look, I'll put a few extra bucks in the basket if you'll knock off that god-awful humming." It would earn more income for the church, but I can't do it. I can't stop humming.

My brother has a quirk that is even more disturbing than my humming. He sings. Not badly; his voice is pleasant enough to tolerate, but like my humming, he sings constantly and everywhere. My brother knows the first line of every song ever written—but only the first line. He never takes the time to learn the second line, or the line after that, or the closing coda. No, he knows only the first line of the song. So that's what he sings. He sings the initial line and then lets the song simply trail off into musical

limbo. Then he sings the first line again . . . and again . . . and again . . .
you get the idea. See, just telling you about it is irritating. Listening to it
incessantly is worse. However, he does have the consideration to change
the song bimonthly.

Can you imagine if Frank Sinatra had this same practice? He'd come
onstage after his introduction to hoots, hollers, and applause. The band
would be playing his theme music. He'd probably raise his glass and toast
the crowd, then his magical, musical voice would sing the first line of his
latest hit. Then he'd sing that first line again . . . and again . . . and again . . .
well, you get the picture (again). If he did this, he probably never would
have become the legendary entertainer that he did.

Here's another trait that gets my goat: Once again, it has to do with
music, which appears to be a pet peeve of mine. For instance, I dislike
restaurants that insist on playing loud, repetitive, irritating music while
you're trying to enjoy a pleasant meal and conversation with friends. If I
want music, I go to a concert. If I want to chat with friends, I go to a quiet
bistro. Intrusive music does not make for a "quiet bistro." If I ask the waiter, waitress, or manager to turn the volume down, it seems they turn it up.
I want peace and quiet; they seek vengeance.

But back to this other trait that gets my goat. An acquaintance of mine
loves to sing. He prides himself on knowing lots of old songs. Unlike my
previously mentioned brother, this gentleman knows the entire song—
every verse of every song. He doesn't consider a song sung until each word
of the lyric has been completed.

Additionally, he can convert almost anything anyone says to a song
lyric. If it's an exact quote of a song lyric, he's deliriously happy. For instance, if you say, "I'm in the mood for lunch," he will launch into the song
"I'm in the Mood for Love." If you say, "I'll grab my coat and go with you,"
he'll put his baritone to work singing "On the Sunny Side of the Street." He
will vocalize for your pleasure until you can't stand it any longer. And once
he begins a song lyric, he's impossible to stop. Once, I said to him, "I think
you hit your ball somewhere over the hill," and he sang "Somewhere Over
the Rainbow." He sang every single lyric of that ballad. He sang verses that

weren't in the movie—verses that not even Judy Garland had ever heard before. If you say, "Knock it off, will you?" the word "off" in the phrase will set him off and he'll begin to sing "Off We Go into the Wild Blue Yonder." It's unknown how many official verses there are in that tune, but when this friend sings it, it seems to last longer than the normal Air Force enlistment period.

Consequently, when playing golf with him, we tend to censor our own speech. We make a concerted effort to not say anything which might be translated into song. It's almost impossible to maintain such diligence. As a result, many of us, when in his company, tend to converse in panto-mime. We say absolutely nothing and pretend we're playing charades.

It still doesn't work. After trying this for several minutes, he catches on and sings "Silent Night."

I have used an insidious revenge plan against this gentleman on occa-sion. As we part company and he is in his car about to drive off, I'll say, "Oh, look at that."

He'll say, "Look at what?"

I'll say, "Oh, nothing. I thought for a minute there I saw ninety-nine bottles of beer on the wall."

I allow him to drive off. Let him annoy himself singing that abomina-ble song for two or three hours.

Continuing along with the musical theme, the finger-tapper can also be disquieting. No wait, I'll change that—he can also be irritating. This is the guy who is continually tapping his fingernails on the desk, on a tabletop, on any surface that is hard enough to produce noticeable clickety-click-click. He taps out rhythms to music he hears on the radio or in his own head. From the wrist down, this guy thinks he's Fred Astaire.

There are two other friends who would often join my wife and me for din-ner. When they did, I can truthfully confess that I would have preferred to be an island. It was supposed to be a democratic arrangement—they would select the restaurant for one meeting; we would select the restau-rant for the next. What could possibly go wrong with such a congenial arrangement as this?

Each time we met at their selected eatery, they pointed out how superb the cuisine was. They told us that they personally knew either the owner or the maître d' and that he or she would arrange for us to have the most desirable table and might also provide complimentary wine, after-dinner cordials, or both for our pleasure. In short, they presented this as the utmost in prestigious dining. We felt privileged to be included.

When they joined us at the restaurant we selected, the drive was always too far, parking was always impossible, and the veal was always fatty. This tests one's patience.

Could I be wrong for allowing so many people to annoy me? Could I possibly be the curmudgeon who is at fault? My spouse often says that I am. She may be absolutely right, but if she says it too many more times, I may add her to the list. You see, this man *wants* to be an island.

I also despise hyperbole. We all know the fisherman's story about the gigantic fish he caught during his last vacation. It was a pretty big fish, and we were happy to hear the story of what a struggle it was to hook it, fight it, and land it. We all expect, too, that each time the fisherman tells that tale, the fish gets larger and larger. We can accept that. It's human nature. Well, it's the part of human nature that goes fishing.

However, some of my friends can convert the fisherman's fib into each story they tell. Fine, if you want to tell me about your niece's nine-year-old son who plays small fry football and is the quarterback of the team that won the league championship, I'm happy to hear it . . . for awhile.

But don't tell me that he's the best player in the league, that he's the best player in the state, that he's the best player who ever played in this league. And definitely don't tell me that his coach has told his parents that he can almost guarantee that he will, if he sticks with it, become a professional football player.

Don't tell me that he can run faster than all the other kids in his class. Don't tell me that he can throw the ball seventy-five yards on the fly. Don't tell me that he can throw the ball seventy-five yards downfield and then run down and catch it himself for an unassisted touchdown.

Don't tell me that he also kicks the extra points (I sort of figured he would, anyway). Don't tell me that he hasn't missed a field goal in seven years. That's an incredible accomplishment for a nine-year-old football player.

Don't tell me that he invented the "Statue of Liberty" play.

I'm not going to believe any of this stuff anyway, so why bother to tell me? It's just something else that irritates me.

Here's another one that's tough, at least for me, to take:

"Hey, I saw a great movie the other day. It was called *The Blue Violet*."

I say, "Yeah, I saw it. It was great."

"It was a great movie."

"Yeah, I know. I saw it."

"You should go see it."

"I saw it."

"It starts out with this guy who is a spy for the CIA."

"I saw the movie."

"The part was played by . . . oh, I can't think of his name."

"It was Tom Cruise."

"He's a famous actor."

"It was Tom Cruise when I saw the movie."

"Oh, well, I'll think of it later. Anyway, he meets this girl."

"I saw the movie."

"And guess what?"

"She turns out to be a spy, too."

"Well, I don't want to tell you. In case you want to go see the movie, you know."

"I saw the movie."

No matter how many times I tell this guy that I saw the movie, he insists on telling me the story of the movie—except, of course, for those parts that I shouldn't know about in case I ever want to see the movie . . . again.

Maybe it's just me, but this irritates me.

I'm funny in a way, too, but I also enjoy ordering my own meal in a restaurant. If the crab cakes sound good and I'm in the mood for crab cakes, I order the crab cakes. If the sand dabs are more appealing, I'll ask for the sand dabs. If a chocolate shake and a cheeseburger are the most appetizing to me at the moment, bring me a cheeseburger with a black and white milkshake—oh yeah, and a side of curly fries with that. Whatever the waiter brings is what I want. It's what I look forward to enjoying.

I don't need any more advice besides what's written on the menu. But certain of my friends will give me that unasked-for advice, unasked for.

"Do you know how many calories are in that burger?"

"No."

"Do you know what that can do to the insides of your arteries?"

"No."

"Are you aware of the problems that obesity is causing in this country?"

"No."

"Do you know they can make a vegetable burger that's just as tasty as that vicious piece of beef?"

"No."

"I just wonder why you're ordering such an unhealthy meal, that's all."

"Well, then, I have a question for you."

"Yes?"

"Do you know that 48 percent of the people who tell other people what's not healthy for them to eat get beaten up before they pay their check?"

"Well, I never . . ."

"Well, good. Don't do it again."

Boy, this milkshake is delicious.

So you see, even though the self-help advocates warn us that no man is an island, some of us might prefer to be one. If you, like me, are one of those, come and live with me in a cave. I'll be easy to find. I'll be in the cave with the humming coming from it.

CHAPTER TWENTY-THREE

PERSISTENCE

"It takes twenty years to make an overnight success."
—Eddie Cantor

Very few traits are promoted as diligently as perseverance. Famed philosopher Julie Andrews noted, "Perseverance is failing nineteen times and succeeding on the twentieth." She never went on to explain what would happen should you fail twenty times. I suppose it's assumed that you would succeed on the twenty-first try. Even renowned philosopher Yogi Berra chipped in with "The game's not over till it's over." Then, too, there's the quote of USMC General O. P. Smith who said, "Retreat—hell! We're not retreating; we're just advancing in a different direction." Even though he may have extended the logic beyond its breaking point, you can readily see how devoted most people are to the concept of perseverance.

The idea has been ingrained in us since childhood. Remember the lessons we were supposed to take from the story of *The Little Engine that Could* and the fable about *The Tortoise and the Hare*. We hear it constantly and from all directions.

"Winners never quit, and quitters never win."

"C'mon, batter. It only takes one."

"It's not how many times you're knocked down but how many times you get up again."

"If at first you don't succeed, try, try again."

"It doesn't matter how slowly you go, so long as you do not stop."

"You've still got gas in the tank."

"You've got to have heart."

"Nobody likes a quitter."

"You can't keep a good man down."

"Give it all you've got."

"You can't quit now."

And this one that you hear from the commentators about a boxer who is being bloodied and battered: "You can't say this kid doesn't have heart." With the bashing he's been taking, that may be all he has left. Yet he's still praised for it.

We call it by many names: perseverance, persistence, determination, tenacity, resolution, endurance, spirit, heart, stick-to-it-iveness, doggedness, hanging in there, stubbornness . . . wait a minute . . . there it is—STUBBORNESS. Finally, a word that we senior citizens can embrace. If anything, we've learned over the years to be stubborn. And we have many words for that, too: obstinate, unyielding, uncompromising, strong willed, mule headed, pigheaded, bullheaded (and probably a few other animal headeds). We excel in all of those.

Those of us who have put in a few years of struggle aren't tempted that fiercely to give up now. We've all passed that point of no return. Through the years, we've been knocked down many times. We've all been belted, blindsided, bombarded, bashed, bopped, bumped, and beleaguered (and any other "B" words you might want to add to that list). After a while, you get used to it.

There's a story told about Bernard Baruch that illustrates the determination of seniors. Baruch was being interviewed on the occasion of his ninety-fifth birthday. He announced there that one of his projects would be to learn to speak Greek. One reporter noted Baruch's advanced age and asked why he had decided to learn Greek now. Mr. Baruch replied, "It's now or never."

Besides, after a certain number of years pursuing our goals, we don't have to quit. We're entitled to a brief rest now and then. Recall the general above who said, "Retreat—hell! We're just advancing in a different direction." We mature self-helpers can say, "Quit? Hell! We're just continuing our quest with a little snoring thrown in on the side." Remember the iconic Little Engine who kept repeating, "I think I can . . . I think I can . . . I think I can." Eventually, like all of us, that Engine said, "I think I can take a little nap now and continue this climb later."

One comedian tells a joke about going to a convenience store that had a sign that read OPEN TWENTY-FOUR HOURS. When he got there, the proprietor was locking the place up. The comic said, "I thought you were open twenty-four hours." The man said, "Not in a row."

Those of us who have grown in wisdom (and probably weariness) should be permitted to interrupt our adventure for a little R and R. To our way of thinking, persistence and being sound asleep are not mutually exclusive. Going back to one of those sayings listed at the top of this chapter: "Winners never quit, and quitters never win." But both winners and quitters take a little rest every now and then. That's all we're doing.

Now, some may argue the above philosophy is nothing more than rationalization. We can debate that, if you like, but remember that we more mature self-helpers are experts at stubbornness. We are more obstinate, unyielding, uncompromising, strong willed, mule headed, pigheaded, and bullheaded than any self-help authors. We say, "Bring it on. It would be a pleasure to give you a hands-on lesson in perseverance."

We'll just outlast you. It's like a staring contest. Who will blink first? We old-timers have a definite advantage. Notice that people who are taking a nap rarely blink. You lose.

There are two classes of people who excel in obstinacy—older folks and younger folks. Before you tell a two-year-old "No," you'd better clear the room of anything that's either valuable or breakable—many times including yourself. That's why my wife will never leave me and the grand-children in the same room together without adult supervision.

Bottom line: I approve of the virtue of persistence. I'll join the self-help authors in recommending perseverance. I've practiced it most of my life. When you have the intelligence quotient and the skill sets that I have, you grow accustomed to people telling you that you can't do things. I've learned to listen and ignore. Let me give you one example of how bull-headed I can be.

My wife told me, "You can't do it."

"Yes, I can," I said.

"No, you can't," she insisted.

"I can," I insisted more.

"You can't."

"I can."

"You can't."

"I can."

This silly exchange continued for some time until my wife remem-bered that I was ornery enough to continue it for weeks.

She broke the pattern. She said, "You can't go out and buy a piece of furniture for a new mother's nursery."

"Look," I said. "My daughter is having my first grandchild, and I want to buy the crib for her nursery. So that's what I'm going to do."

"Alone?" she asked.

"All by my lonesome," I said with my bullheaded charm.

My wife said, "Good luck."

Ha! How much luck would I need to buy a crib?

The saleswoman at the store looked very friendly, knowledgeable, and grandmotherly. This was going to be a piece of cake . . . I thought.

"May I help you?" she said.

"Yes. I'd like to buy a crib."

"All by yourself?" she asked.

I looked around to see why she asked that question. No one else was there, so she must have been talking to me.

"Yes," I said.

"Why me?" she muttered, more to herself than to me.

I said, "It's for my daughter, who is having my first grandchild." I was proud and I wanted her to be a part of that.

She didn't seem to be thrilled at that, nor did she seem thrilled to have to be waiting on me. Instead, she got down to business. "What is she doing the nursery in?" she asked.

"You mean 'What is she going to be doing in the nursery?'" I said, thinking she had misspoken.

Apparently she didn't. She repeated, "No, what is she doing the nursery in?"

I said, "I don't know what that means."

"How is she going to decorate it?" she explained.

That explained nothing to me. I said, "I have no idea."

"Don't you think you should find out?" she asked.

"Why? I said. "I'm just buying a crib, not the whole nursery."

This woman was clever enough to know that she was dealing with above-average stubbornness here, so she said resignedly, "Okay. What color crib do you want?"

Feeling that I was beginning to gain the upper hand in this battle, I said smugly, "What color cribs do you have?"

She returned my smugness with her own smugness. "We have every color you can imagine, sir."

I said, "Don't you have a basic crib color?"

She said, "Sir, there is no such thing as a basic crib color. It has to match the décor." Now she was starting to patronize me.

I would have none of it, though. (Remember, I was persistent.) I replied with a clever retort. I said, "Why?"

"Look," she said, "if you had a blue pinstriped suit, would you want me to buy you an orange tie with green checks to go with it?"

I said, "Of course not."

She shrugged her shoulders as if to say, *Well, there you have it.*

I said, "I already have an orange tie with green checks to go with my blue pinstriped suit."

"You'd better find out what she's doing the nursery in," she advised.

I excused myself to call my wife.

I returned and told the saleswoman proudly, "She's doing the nursery in green."

"What color green?" she asked.

"Green is a color," I said.

She said, "Not quite. There's kelly green, forest green, lime green, mint green . . ."

I said, "How about baby green?"

"There's no such thing as baby green," she said.

"Well, you have lime green, mint green, and forest green. My daughter's having a baby, not a plant."

She just stared at me defiantly.

But I could be defiant too. So I left again and went to call my wife.

When I came back, the sales clerk was waiting for me with arms folded—definitely a defensive stance.

But I was ready to initiate my offense. "We're doing the nursery in lime green," I said.

"Oh, we are?" She emphasized the "we" with a bit of sarcasm, as if to imply that surely I had no part in the decision.

I didn't, but I was too hardheaded to admit that. I said, "Yes, we are." Now I emphasized the "we" with a touch of *Don't mess with me, babe, because I'm a tiger when I'm pushed too far.*

"Now," I said, "may I see some cribs?"

"And what's the theme of the nursery?" she asked.

"What theme?" I said. "What are you talking about?"

"The theme," she said. "The theme." As if saying it two, three, or four times would make it more understandable.

"I don't know what a theme is," I confessed.

She enjoyed that. She was like a boxer who had the opponent whipped and now was just throwing in a couple of body shots as added punishment.

"I didn't think you would," she said. "Anyone who thinks there's only one green certainly wouldn't know what a theme is."

"Could you be so kind as to tell me?"

"A theme, a theme," she said. (Again with the condescending repetitive statements. Like Einstein could have made us all understand his theories by simply saying, "Relativity, relativity.") But she went on. "A theme is like whether she's going to decorate the room in bunny rabbits or cute little duckies. Is she going to do it with clown faces or little baby angels?"

"Do I really need to know the theme?" I asked.

"Yes, you really do." This woman was merciless.

"Why?" I whined. Then I answered my own dumb question. "I know. Because if I had a suit that was covered with little yellow duckies, you wouldn't want to buy me a tie with pink bunny rabbits."

She didn't respond, which meant, "You got it."

I asked, "You don't just have a neutral cartoon figure that goes with everything?"

"Of course not," she said.

I said, "I'll be back." I had to go to call my wife.

When I returned, I said, "My daughter's doing the nursery in Winnie the Pooh."

"Pooh?" she said.

"Yes," I said. "Winnie the."

"Pooh," she repeated. I sensed that she wasn't happy with me for some reason or another.

"Pooh," I reiterated.

She said (very patronizingly, I might add), "Sir, we have at least four different Winnie the Poohs in our collection. You have your classic Pooh, your Disney Pooh . . ."

I cut her off right there. "I can't do this," I said and turned to leave.

But I did hear her mutter as I was walking away, "That's the first thing you got right since you came in."

Some of you may object that this tale doesn't really illustrate persistence at all. In fact, I surrendered. Let me point out that there is another aspect of persistence that is often overlooked by the dedicated self-helpers: "changing your mind." Suppose, for example, you decide that you want to try skydiving. Friends encourage you to forge ahead with that goal. Pursue it, they tell you. And you do. You make arrangements, take whatever training is necessary, book your first jump, climb into the airplane, reach the correct altitude, step to the open door. All you have to do now is jump. But, instead, you change your mind. You say to yourself, "I think instead of skydiving, I'll pursue square dancing." Good choice. Step out of your chute and go shopping for a pair of jeans and a plaid shirt.

That's how I persisted in the above story. I changed my mind. Instead of buying a crib, I gave my daughter cash. It was money, green on a white background, with pictures of George Washington as the theme. The Gilbert Stuart George Washington, not the classic or the Disney George Washington.

My daughter bought a crib with it.

Persistence—or changing one's mind—pays off.

CHAPTER TWENTY-FOUR

TECHNOLOGY

"It has become appallingly obvious that our technology
has exceeded our humanity." —Albert Einstein

Self-help used to be much simpler in the days of the old-timers. At one time, this philosophy involved your subconscious and your conscious. It was you and whatever shenanigans were going on inside your head. Today, though, it's you, your conscious mind, your subconscious mind, your Facebook page, your Twitter account, your Wi-Fi password, your computer firewall, and whatever other weird devices you have working for or against you.

Napoleon Hill didn't know and didn't want to know about any of this stuff. He just wanted to help you get from where you were to where you wanted to be. Nowadays, though, you can't get anywhere without some sort of device hooked up to you and to some tower that sends out mysterious signals. People today pull out of their driveways and have a smartphone in their ear before the garage door closes.

Even before the days of all the magical computers, tablets, and miraculous phones, I had an employer ask me to get a pager. (For those of you too young to remember, a pager was a device that you hooked on your belt that would buzz when someone wanted to reach you.) I told my employer "No."

He asked why.

I said, "I don't want anything else on my body that could fall off."

I didn't wear the pager.

If that same employer wanted to reach an employee today, he could just find out where that person is via the GPS system on the person's smartphone and possibly send a drone to either bring him or her back to work or fire him or her.

The new technology is demeaning. This is where we older folks might have a slight advantage. We don't depend on the modern electronic devices. While we were all busy aging, those new devices came and went right by us. We hardly knew they existed until we would go into a restaurant and wonder what tricks all those people were doing with their dexterous thumbs.

Ironically, I rebelled against this digital revolution before it even happened. I was angry at being depersonalized by numbers. I love my name. It's Eugene. It means "well born," and I'm quite proud of it. It's brought me some ridicule over the years because every nerd in every movie that features a nerd is named Eugene.

Gene Autry was no nerd. He could beat up any desperado in the West without even losing his white cowboy hat. Believe me, anyone who could jump off the roof of a two story building, land straddling his horse, and ride off singing a western ballad was no nerd.

If Eugene was good enough for Mr. Autry, it's good enough for me.

Unfortunately, there came a time when none of us got to use our name as much as we would have liked. All of us were reduced to numbers. That continues to this day.

My government loves me and protects me. My forefathers wrote a constitution to protect my liberty and added a bill of rights to further

enhance my freedoms. My ancestors fought valiantly to win indepen-
dence for me. Our officials boast that this is a government of the people,
by the people, and for the people. To that same government today, I'm
known by my social security number or my voter registration number. If
I called the president and said, "Hi, this is Gene, and I would like to visit
you at the White House, talk to you, and get to know you better," I'd have
another number added to the list—my secret service file number.

I recently joined a country club in my new neighborhood, not so much
for the golf but for the social benefits. I wanted to go "where everybody
knows my name," as the *Cheers* theme song used to say. It didn't work.

To the guy who shines the shoes in the locker room, I'm locker #421.
To the bartender and the waiters in the club lounge, I'm tab #6133. To the
caddies, I'm bag #715, and to the guys I play with, I'm my handicap. "You
don't want to play with him. He's a thirty-one."

I recently tried to buy a soft canvas briefcase with my name embla-
zoned on the side. I wanted to carry around something that was important
to me that also proclaimed that my name is "Gene." So I called a mail
order company.

The first thing the person at the other end of the phone asked was,
"May I have your customer ID number, please?"

I said, "No."

She said, "No?"

I said, "No."

She said, "Who do you think you are?"

I said, "*I* know who I am. I want *you* to know who I am."

She said, "Give me your customer ID number and I'll know who
you are."

I said, "How about if I just give you my name along with a brief de-
scription of who I am and what I've done with my life?"

She said, "If you'll just give me the three-digit number shown on the
back of your catalog, I'll know all that."

So I relented and gave her my customer ID number.

She said, "There, that wasn't so hard, was it?"

I said, "You're impertinent for a customer service representative."

She said, "And you're arrogant for a guy with a thirty-one handicap." (She could tell that from my customer ID number?)

She asked, "Should I send this to 3319 Suchandsuch Road?"

I said, "No. That's my old address. I've moved."

She said, "May I have your new address please?"

I told her, "993 Soandso Drive."

She said, "Zip code?"

I gave it to her—another number.

She said, "That's in Sunnyville, California."

I said, "No, it's not. It's in Palm Creek, California."

She said, "My computer shows that zip code as Sunnyville."

I said, "It's Palm Creek."

She said, "When I punch your zip code in, it gives me Sunnyville."

I said, "When I drive to my house each night, I drive to Palm Creek. My wife and kids greet me, and guess what? They call me by my name, not my customer ID number."

She said, "We're sending this shipment to Sunnyville."

I said, "Then find someone in Sunnyville who is willing to pay for it, because I don't want it."

I hung up.

To my mailman, I'm a PO Box number. To my bank, I'm an account number. To my favorite department store, I'm a credit card number. To my union, I'm a membership number. To my lawyer, I'm a case number. To my doctor, I'm an insurance number.

About the only place I go where numbers aren't the order of the day is a restaurant. It's refreshing when a person says, "Hi, I'm Michael. I'll be your waiter for the evening."

And to Michael, I'm not a number. Because when Michael brings the plates, he says to me, "Let's see . . . you're the New York steak medium well, right?"

No, Michael, I'm Gene.

There was an age of innocence in the self-help genre. There was a time when you were you and the only one responsible for you and your achievements was you. It was a time of zero tolerance in the self-improvement community. You either achieved or you didn't. You either made it or you fell by the wayside. Nowadays, those newfangled contraptions all come with "achievement aids." My father used to say to me, "You know what's wrong with you, Son? You don't know where your head's at." Nowadays, every son knows where his head is at. The GPS on his smartphone tells him.

But rather than aid us in our quest for a goal, the technology can be counterproductive. It can offer us digitalized excuses for our lack of accomplishment. Rather than plan, practice, and struggle to attain our goals, we'd rather have a rationale for not reaching them. All of us would like to have at the ready some prefabricated excuse, a rationale that we could use to explain away any and all of our faults, mistakes, indiscretions, or lack of industry. We'd like to be able to say, "I didn't amount to anything, but it wasn't my fault. The battery was low on my iPhone."

There was once a king, probably apocryphal, who challenged the wise men in his domain (they were most likely apocryphal, also) to come up with a wise saying that could be used for any occasion or event. The ruler wanted to appear sagacious without going to the trouble of learning how to do it.

The winning entry was, "This, too, shall pass away." It did apply in every instance, but that was also its downfall. The king began using the saying as much as some of our contemporaries use the phrase "You know."

The queen said to him one day, "King, you say one phrase an awful lot, and it's becoming annoying."

The king said, "My dear, this, too, shall pass away."

She said, "That's the phrase I'm talking about."

Even his subjects became irritated. When they complained about taxation, oppressive laws, and cruel treatment at the hands of his soldiers, the monarch always had the same universal response.

Finally, they overthrew his government, brought him to the scaffold, and asked for his final words. He said, "This, too, shall pass away." And with those words, he did.

This is a saying that's always applicable, but it doesn't always do you a lot of good. For instance, an officer pulls you over on the highway:

"I'd like to see your license and registration. You were doing seventy-five miles an hour in a forty-five-mile zone."

"Well, officer, this, too, shall pass away."

"Alright, wise guy, outta the car . . ."

I had a nearly perfect saying when I was a kid that got me out of considerable trouble. It was a one-word question: "What?" It was most effective when spoken with a tone of confusion or surprise.

My mother would say, "Young man, I want to talk to you."

I'd say, "What?"

"Exactly where were you last night?"

"What?"

"And who were you with?"

"What?"

"You know exactly what I'm talking about."

"What?"

"Did you think you could get away with it?"

"What?"

Finally, Mom would get frustrated and say, "Oh, go on. Get out of here."

Adults have a very low tolerance of about six to eight "What"s.

Of course, the gimmick didn't work so well when I reached adulthood.

My boss called me into his office and said, "I think you know what I want to talk about."

I said, "What?"

He said, "Production in your department is down, and I'd like to know why."

I said, "What?"

He said, "You're fired."

I said, "WHAT??!!"

Since then, I've abandoned the phrase that served me so well in my early life.

Clever minds, though, and advancing technology have finally discovered an excuse that serves as a response for any complaint, request, whatever. It's very simple: "Our computers are down."

Here's an example of how it works:

One time, an airline clerk issued me an incorrect ticket, so I immediately tried to rectify it.

"Excuse me," I said, "But I asked for a ticket to Oakland and you've issued me one to Auckland."

The clerk replied, "I'm sorry, but I can't help you, sir. Our computers are down."

I said, "What am I supposed to do?"

"I'd suggest you fly to Auckland and maybe their computers will be operating."

I said, "But isn't Auckland in New Zealand?"

The clerk said, "I have no way of knowing, sir. Our computers are down."

The phrase works on the telephone, too. I called a mail order company to inquire about an order I'd placed. "I'd like to know when I might expect my package to arrive."

"I'm sorry," the other end of the phone said. "Our computers are down."

"But I sent in my $19.95 two months ago and haven't received anything yet."

"Sir, our records show nothing about receiving $19.95 from you."

"I thought your computers were down."

"Just that one is working."

This new universal excuse even applies where it has no business applying, like in buying a wedding gift for a friend.

I said to the sales clerk, "I don't know much about buying wedding gifts, but this is a close friend and I'd like to get something nice. Maybe you could help me."

She said, "No, I can't. Our computers are down."

I said, "What does that have to do with any—"

"When the bride and groom register at our store, we put them on our computer. Now our computer is down."

"Then just sell me something."

"That wouldn't be right. Then the bride and groom might get several gifts they don't want."

So this way they don't get any gifts, because the computer is down.

There's one time this near-universal excuse doesn't work—when *you* try to use it.

The electric company called and warned me that my bill was overdue, and if it wasn't paid soon, I'd lose power.

I said, "Well, I'm sorry. I'd like to pay you immediately, but you see, my computer is down."

The lights went out.

But that's all right. I figure this, too, shall pass away.

We old-timers realize that Christopher Columbus stumbled upon a new world without the use of a GPS system, the Internet, or an iPhone connected to the Cloud. If he could do it on his own, so can you and I.

CHAPTER TWENTY-FIVE

SELF-DISCIPLINE

"The only way to get rid of temptation is to yield to it ... I can resist everything but temptation." —Oscar Wilde

W hat is self-discipline? The teachers in the early grades taught us that self-discipline was all about the hands. They would instruct us to sit quietly with our hands folded before us. We were not to move, not to talk, and not to chew gum—above all, not to chew gum. Gum, to these teachers, was the devil incarnate. It was the personification of all the evil in the world. No one who mastered self-discipline ever chewed gum. No human should chew gum anywhere, especially not in the classroom. If these teachers found you chewing gum, they would force you to remove it from your mouth and place it on the tip of your nose. It would remain there for the rest of the school day. Of course, it looked silly there, so you became the laughingstock of the entire class. Well, not really the entire class, because about 85 percent of the other kids also had gum stuck on their noses.

It was ironic, though, because these same teachers preached that "idle hands were the devil's workshop." Yet when they wanted to teach us self-control, they had us fold our hands demurely in front of us. What could be idler than hands with fingers interlocked just sitting there, not permitted to do anything? Make up your mind. Are idle hands good or bad? Do they promote mischief or do they epitomize self-discipline?

I suppose it worked. It certainly encouraged self-control. It's extremely difficult to do anything naughty without using your hands. Surely, there are possibilities, but we early graders weren't clever enough to think of them. But that's probably why police handcuff criminals. The police learned in school, just as we did, that immobilized hands promote acceptable behavior. Although, most criminals can still chew gum, but that's a different argument.

"Discipline" is a confusing and contradictory concept. Often discipline implies a punishment. Going back to our school days again, if you unfolded your hands or spoke out of turn, or if you were caught chewing gum, you might be sent to the "disciplinarian." That was trouble. That meant you would be disciplined, which meant punishment. "Discipline" in that sense was a bad thing.

But discipline also denotes self-control. It indicates that you can follow orders—that you can do the right thing at the right time. It represents commendable behavior. So, is discipline a good thing or a bad thing? Who knows?

The self-help philosophy presents self-discipline as a virtue. In fact, they tout it as an indispensable trait. Success, achievement, and accomplishments are impossible if you insist on being lackadaisical, lazy, or a laggard. (Notice that self-helpers also seem to enjoy alliteration.) To succeed, it seems, a person must be resigned to doing what must be done whether they're inclined at the moment to do it or not. It means working when you'd rather not. It implies studying when you'd rather not. It means keeping your shoulder to the wheel, your nose to the grindstone, and your head held high. If you can continue to do all that, you will reach your goal, but once you get there, it's going to be hard to find a suit that fits your newly misshapen body.

There's another irony of the self-help propaganda—they promote all achievement as very achievable. If you think it's so, it will be so. If you can picture it, it will happen. If you wish hard enough, you will accomplish. Everything is easy. Yet they promote self-discipline. In other words, you must be strong enough to do all that easy stuff.

Let's simplify the definition of self-discipline: if you don't want to do it, you should do it. We all endured this as children, although it was hardly self-discipline. It was more like parent-induced-discipline.

"Mom, I'm going over to the park. We have a ball game at two o'clock."

"Young man, you're going to march into the parlor and practice your piano lessons for one solid hour."

"But Mom, the game'll be over by then."

"Good. Then you can stay home and practice for another half hour."

"Aw, Mom..."

I am Mr. Middle C, take a good long look at me . . . ad infinitum (it seemed).

Or:

"Mom, I'm going over to Billy's house."

"Young man, you're going to march upstairs and finish your homework."

"But Mom, all the other kids are going to Billy's house."

"If all the other kids were going to jump off a bridge, would you do it, too?"

"If the bridge was on the way to Billy's house, I would."

"Don't be impertinent, young man. Just get in your room and do your homework."

"Aw, Mom..."

Two times three is six . . . *three times three is nine* . . . *four times three is twelve* . . . ad infinitum again.

Or:

"Mom, I'm going to the movies . . ."

"No, you're not."

"But, Mom, what do I have to do now?"

"I don't know, but I'll think of something."

That's how we grew up to appreciate self-discipline. It was relatively easy when we were young. Our moms or dads did all the planning and enforcing. We simply had to complain and comply. It became more difficult as we matured and attended college. That introduced the "self" into self-discipline, as in this example from a wide-eyed freshman:

"I don't think I'll be going out with you tonight."

"What do you mean?"

"Well, I have to cram for a very difficult calculus exam. And I'm way behind in my argumentation and effective reasoning course. I'm afraid I'm in for an all-nighter on that one."

"Yeah, but the Gamma Delta frat is having a wild toga party tonight."

"Why didn't you say so? Let's go."

Well, maybe the "self" didn't do such a good job during college. Of course, after college came boss-discipline, girlfriend-discipline, spouse-discipline, taking-care-of-the-kids-discipline, and on and on and on.

Even after we retired, our discipline wasn't determined by ourselves. It was decided more by how late we could stay up, what kind of foods we could eat without heartburn, how well our bodies could or couldn't move, and just how interested we were in what we were doing to convince ourselves that we should do it well. After a certain age, self-discipline was reduced to remembering to take the right pills at the right time.

Is self-discipline really controlled by oneself? Probably not. Is self-discipline vital in achieving goals? Probably not as much as they say it is. Is it effective at all as a success tool? Much evidence seems to indicate that it isn't. Infants probably have the least self-discipline of anyone. If they feel like crying, they cry. If they want to throw a tantrum, they throw a tantrum. If anything makes them uncomfortable, they wail away. Self-discipline is not an infant's strong suit.

Nevertheless, babies boast of a success rate that would put the rest of us to shame. If an infant wakes up bawling at two or three o'clock in the morning, what happens? The mother or the father—whichever one is the quickest thinker—nudges the other and says, "Go feed the baby." The nudgee gets up, staggers to the kitchen, warms the young one's bottle, and suddenly realizes: *Why am I doing this? I should have nudged first.*

The youngster doesn't care. It fills its tummy and goes back to a peaceful sleep. That's an example of getting things done, and self-discipline had nothing to do with it. Perhaps we should listen to our offspring instead of our self-help gurus.

Is self-discipline important? Absolutely. It allows us to control some of the evil tendencies we all have. It gives us dominion over the seven deadly sins: lust, gluttony, greed, sloth, envy, pride, and the ever-popular anger. (If you want to add an eighth deadly sin, throw in chewing gum.)

I remember one time when I was angry and should have exercised self-control but didn't. Typically, it was over nothing, or so miniscule to be almost nothing. A friend of mine had a motto: "Don't sweat the small stuff. And remember, everything is the small stuff." I should have followed that wisdom, but I didn't.

I stormed into the house, slamming the door shut behind me. "I'm furious," I said. "Absolutely incensed. I don't think I've been this angry about anything in my life." To punctuate my irritation, I threw a few knickknacks around.

"You seem upset," my wife said. (Women notice things like that.)

"Yes, I'm upset," I said. "I'm very upset. I'm more upsetter than I've ever been in my whole adult life."

My wife said, "I can see. It's even affecting your grammar. What's wrong?"

"Who's my best friend in the entire world?" I asked her.

She said, "I would say Mack is."

"That's right," I said. "Good old Mack. My best friend from the old neighborhood, from the old days. I was best man at his wedding, and he was best man at my wedding."

"Our wedding," my wife corrected me.

"And he is number one on the memory dialing on our phone, right?"

"No. Mack is number five on our phone."

"Well, sure. Our four kids are ahead of him, but he's the first person on our memory dialing who is not a product of our loins, right?"

"I wouldn't phrase it quite that way, but yes, he is. Why does that annoy you so much?"

"Because I'm not on his memory dialing at all."

"Really?" she said.

"Yes, really. I'm supposed to be his best friend in the entire world, and he has the audacity to dial me manually."

"That's outrageous," she said.

I said, "Well, I'm glad you agree with me." (I had totally missed the sarcasm of her comment.) "I want him out of our will."

"I don't think he's in our will."

"Well, put him in there and then take him out. That'll show him."

"Indeed. That'll be excruciatingly painful revenge." My spouse didn't seem to be giving this episode the intensity it clearly deserved. "Don't you think you're overreacting?"

I said, "Not at all. This is a personal affront."

"Oh, come on," she said.

"There are fifteen buttons on his memory dialing. I counted them."

"So?"

"So," I explained as patiently as I could in my infuriated state, "he's my best friend in the entire world, and I'm not even in his top fifteen."

She said, "You're being silly."

"I don't care," I said. "I definitely want him out of the will."

She said, "He's not in the will." Then she added, "Why don't you put him in the will and leave him a telephone that has thirty memory-dialing buttons on it?"

I said, "You think this is funny, don't you?"

"A little bit," she admitted.

"I get metaphorically slapped in the face by my best friend in the entire world, and you think it's a big joke."

She said, "What are you going to do now? Take me out of the will?"

"Well, I'm going to do something to get even with him, I'll tell you that right now."

"Don't get crazy. Control yourself."

"I got it!" I shouted, ignoring her advice. "You know that number we never call anymore? The insurance company that we dropped?"

My wife said, "Yeah." She glanced at our phone and said, "They're number eleven on our machine."

I said, "Well, I'm going to put him after them. How about that, huh? He'll be lower than a number we never even call."

My wife said, "This may sound dumb, but if we never call that number, why is it on our memory dialing?"

I said, "Because I don't know how to get rid of it. That's why."

She said, "This may sound dumber, but if you don't know how to get rid of that number, how are you going to get rid of his?"

"I'll learn!" I shouted. "I'll learn."

"No, you won't," she said.

Her honest logic infuriated me even more. "Then I'll buy a new phone and put the number we never call back in and then put him after it."

"You're being totally irrational."

"You don't understand the impact of this insult. Would Butch Cassidy get upset if the Sundance Kid didn't have him on his memory dialing? How about Huck Finn? He'd get steamed if Tom Sawyer didn't have him on memory dialing. Antony and Cleopatra. Abbott and Costello. I could go on forever."

My wife said, "I think you could. And that's why I'm going to put an end to this."

She picked up the phone.

"What are you doing?" I asked.

She said, "I'm calling Mack." She pushed button five on our phone—the first one after our beloved children.

She said into the phone, "Hiya, Mack. It's Sally. I'm doing good. And you? Listen, do me a favor, will you? Put our number on your memory dialing. Oh, it's already on there? It's number one? Gene said he looked at your phone and didn't see it listed. Oh, I see." She covered the mouthpiece and said to me, "It's listed as MBF. That stands for 'My Best Friend.'"

She spoke back into the phone. "Thanks, Mack. He'll feel better about that. Bye." She hung up.

She said to me, "Are you happy now?"

I said, "I'm number one?"

She said, "That's right."

I said, "Listed as 'My Best Friend?'"

"Just like Butch and Sundance."

"That Mack is a great guy, isn't he? You know what? I'm going to move him up to number one on our phone."

She said, "That would be nice." (She knew I'd never be able to learn how to do it.)

So we all need self-discipline—maybe not to become a success, but just to become a better person.

CHAPTER TWENTY-SIX

HOW TO GET PEOPLE TO LIKE YOU

"He has no enemies, but is intensely disliked by his friends."
—Oscar Wilde

Self-help literature advocates learning how to get people to like you. Being congenial, gracious, and charming are stepping stones, so they say, to meaningful achievement. That may be so, but those of us who have a few miles on the odometer have become curmudgeonly. For the most part, we don't want people to like us; we want people to leave us alone.

But besides just being grouchy old scoundrels, we have other reasons to be skeptical of this principle. The self-help experts prompt us to be pleasant, outgoing, and friendly. They advise that we smile more and deliberately try to make others feel more important when they're around us.

It's all in an effort to win associates over to our way of thinking. In other words, it's a con game. Those of us who have a few years to our credit seem to be more vulnerable to deception, so we're skeptical of anything that smells of a scam. Getting people to like us has that scam-like aroma.

It borders on trickery. We want to appear friendly, concerned for others, solicitous of their needs—all of this so that we can get what we want from them. Basically, we're concerned and solicitous of our own needs, not theirs. Isn't that deceptive?

One family complained that after their son had gone off to college, he never wrote. The parents said he never even answered the letters they sent to him. The boy's grandmother said, "I'll write to him, and I'll get a response almost immediately." They hardly believed her.

Later, she showed them his response to her letter. They were amazed and wanted to know how she did it. She said, "I wrote him a nice letter asking how college was going, if he was enjoying it, and so on and so forth. However, I did add a PS that said, 'I hope you enjoy the check I enclosed and spend the money wisely.'"

His response letter answered all of her questions but also noted that she must have forgotten to include the check.

A bit of a subterfuge, but we can forgive a clever, caring grandmother. Trickery, though, for pure self-advancement is not so easily condoned. The self-helpers seem to be attempting to turn all of us into conmen. "I want to do all I can to help all of you get exactly what I want."

They advise that we master the art of diplomacy. One facet of that, they teach, is to never tell anyone that they are wrong. But what if they are wrong? Should we let a driver continue to drive the wrong way on the interstate simply because it would be demoralizing and harmful to his self-esteem if we shouted "Turn around, you numbskull! You're going to get somebody hurt!" Perhaps there is a more diplomatic way to inform him, but inform him we should.

They also suggest that we should be humble. It makes us more accepted by others. We become less of a challenge to their own self-image. This feels contradictory. So much of the improvement literature has told us to build our confidence, heighten our self-esteem, think proudly of ourselves and our goals. Now we're told to be humble.

Listen to the self-helpers: "You can be rich, famous, powerful. You can have anything at all that you want. No quest is too impossible for you, you humble, groveling, little good-for-nothing." Make up your mind, please. Are we invincible or are we eminently vincible?

Self-helpers teach this principle for a self-serving reason. The theory is that a big reason for success is a person's interaction with others. It's not necessarily your training, your talents, your skills, or your expertise. They claim that's about 15 percent of the reason. The real reason for most achievement, they say, is how you present yourself to others. If you're affable and amusing, that amounts to the other 85 percent of your success.

Let's personalize this and see how well it translates:

Suppose your dishwasher is acting up. It's over ten years old. It has served you well during that time, but now it's rebelling. Should you call a repairman who knows what he's doing? You can if you want, but the self-helpers indicate that you'd be more likely to select a clueless repairman with a warm, friendly smile and sexy dimples. He'll come to the house with his toolbox and amuse you with delightful tales and playful banter. He's wonderful, and you enjoy welcoming him into your house. When he's done, you cheerfully write him a check for $412 and you have a few good laughs with Mr. Personality as your kitchen begins to flood.

Maybe you should have gone with the 15 percenter who knew how to fix a dishwasher.

The experts also advise us: "Don't criticize people." No one enjoys being told that they're wrong. But really, in telling us not to criticize people, aren't they themselves criticizing us for criticizing people? How come they can do it to us, but we can't do it to other people? (I warned you that we older folks get curmudgeonly.)

Besides, what if people are dead wrong? Take, for example, the above-mentioned incompetent but convivial dishwasher mechanic. You're still bailing water out of the kitchen, and the dishwasher is still broken. Are you expected to say, "Hey, Pally, good job. I'm going to recommend you to all my friends in the neighborhood. They'll enjoy you as much as we have."

Shouldn't we opt for ability over affability? There's a story told about people who know what they're doing as opposed to those who get by on personality:

The late band leader Benny Goodman was traveling with his orchestra, and at one city, he needed a trombonist. He asked the band members if they knew anybody in town who might fill in. One musician volunteered a friend of his who played trombone. Benny Goodman asked if he was any good. The musician said honestly, "He's not real good, but I'll tell you what—he's a fun guy. Terrific personality, very witty, and great to be on the bandstand with." Benny Goodman replied, "Find me a jerk who swings."

The successful authors also advise that you go out of your way to make others feel important. Let's lean on our hapless dishwasher repairman again. "Hey kids, come and meet the delightful dishwasher repairman who built the lovely swimming pool in our kitchen." That should make him feel good.

Self-help authors also propose that you talk to people about what they want rather than what you want. Let's see how effective that is:

Suppose you have a nagging cough that's been bothering you all morning. You finally stop at a drugstore to get some soothing cough drops. The owner behind the counter greets you warmly. "Good morning, sir, is there anything you want?"

"Yes, there is, but I'd much rather talk about what you want." Cough, cough. "Wouldn't you like a brand new car?"

Taken aback, the owner says, "Yes, I would, but I can't really afford it right now. But can I get something for you?"

"Forget about me for a minute." Cough, cough. "If I helped you increase your business, maybe you could afford that new car." Cough, cough. "Would you like that?"

"We're not doing badly here. We'll get by."

"I'm sure you will, but if you could get a new car"—cough, cough—"what one would you like?"

"I don't know. I'd have to ask the wife." He shouts toward the back of the store, "Helen, can you come here a minute?"

She arrives. "Yes?"

"What kind of a car do you want?"

She says, "What?"

"What kind of a car do you want?"

She says, "I don't want a car."

You say, "Madam, a new car is a definite possibility." Cough, cough. "Don't dismiss it lightly. And . . . if there's anything I can do to help you acquire it, you let me know." Cough, cough. And with that, you leave.

The druggist says to his wife, "He seemed strange, but a nice guy."

She says, "Yes, he was pleasant enough, but he should do something about that cough."

Don't you agree he should have talked more about what he wanted and less about what they wanted?

The self-helpers suggest, too, that you not only become interested in others but that you become genuinely interested in others. The key word here is "genuinely." It's difficult to be genuine when everything you're doing is so that you can become rich, famous, and powerful. You want to be genuinely interested in what others want so that you can get what you want.

This is reminiscent of George Burns's famous quote about the importance of sincerity in show business. He said, "If you can learn to fake that, you've got it made."

Other sage advice that the experts offer to influence people is to become a good listener. Listen to people attentively so that you can see their point of view. Why do you want to see their point of view? So that you can more readily convince them of your point of view. In other words, "I will listen to you until I can see that you share my opinion."

I wasn't really good in following this suggestion, either. I would patiently listen to people explaining their opinion. I would try to understand it. Then, as suddenly as lightning, I would proclaim, "I see your point of view. I understand what you're saying. I see it more clearly now. It still sounds stupid." I must confess that didn't get a lot of people to like me.

This whole idea sounds too manipulative. I'll do whatever it takes to show you that what I want doesn't really matter. It's what you want that's important. If I can convince you of that, it's easier for me to get what I want.

One very important aspect of getting people to like you is to know the person's name. People take great pride in their names—I mean, unless your name is Hinkley Humpffrumpf or something like that. But probably even old "Hink" Humpffrumpf would be upset if you mistakenly called him "Hank." This is where I—and I'm sure others in and around my age—have a quarrel with this "Get people to like you" precept. I have a terrible time remembering names. I can meet you, hear your name, shake your hand, and forget your name before the end of the handshake.

Once, I was introduced to a person. He said, "How do you do? I'm Ludwig Huftweight."

I said, "What's your name again?"

He repeated very audibly, "Ludwig Huftweight."

I said, "Ludwig, it's a pleasure to meet you."

We chatted briefly then parted.

My wife asked me, "Who was that you were just chatting with?"

I said, "I have no idea."

It's almost harder to forget Ludwig Huftweight than it is to remember it, but I managed to do just that.

Do you know how you'll sometimes receive junk items in the mail? You tear them up and discard them without even opening them, right? Well, because of some congenital flaw in my thinking processes, I treat names like junk mail. I'm not proud of that. I'm embarrassed by it. But I'm resigned to living with it.

I even went to a psychiatrist to see if he could help me with this problem. His name was Dr. . . . uh . . . well, you can see he didn't help much.

It seems that when I hear a name, it goes in one ear and out the other. Some very famous people have had this same problem. For instance, Vincent van Gogh was the same way, except that later in life, when he heard a name, it went in one ear and out the same one.

Had I created the world and all that's in it, I would have made nametags a part of the human anatomy. We don't need the appendix. No one knows what it does. I would have replaced it with a built-in nametag.

Hi, my name is Kathryn would have done more for mankind than the appendix does. However, our Creator saw things differently, which is understandable. He has a better memory than I do . . . at least for names.

I've tried several gimmicks. Once, I heard that if you repeat the name five times, it will be seared into your memory forever. I tried that.

"John, it's good to see you again." I said. "How have things been with you, John? I was looking forward to seeing you here, John, and now that I've seen you, John, I had to come over and say, 'Hello, John.' Maybe I'll see you again, John. If not, you be sure to have a great time. OK, John?"

Just then John's wife came over. He introduced her to me. "This is my wife, Mabel."

I shook her hand.

She said to her husband, "I hate to interrupt your conversation, but there's someone I want you to meet, Fred."

FRED?

So Fred went off with his wife, whatever her name was. He may be Fred to her, but he'll always and forever be John to me. He has to be. I repeated the name five times, and that's the law.

I've also tried memory aids. The experts advise: "When you meet a person, relate their name to some outstanding physical condition." I met a gentleman named Osgood Hummock. Osgood had a large midsection, so I immediately associated "Hummock" with "stomach." No way now that I would ever forget Osgood's name.

Later, my wife came over and I introduced her. I glanced at Osgood's ample midsection and said, "Honey, have you met Mr. Kelly?"

Be aware that trying to get people to like you is not always a likable trait. Trying to win friends and influence people is a dangerous social endeavor—often a fatal one. People may come to say of you, as Oscar Wilde once said, "He has no enemies, but is intensely disliked by his friends."

CHAPTER TWENTY-SEVEN

MAKING DECISIONS

"No good decision was ever made in a swivel chair."
—George S. Patton Jr.

Decision making is not a skill that is hampered by age. Finally, we've come across something that we older folks can do as well as the whippersnappers. The problem, though, is that even though we can match the younger folks in this area, we older citizens are fed up with decision making. We've been making decisions longer than the youngsters, and we've rebelled. To illustrate, let me tell you about a recent personal event. I took my wife out for a quiet, somewhat romantic dinner.

The maître d' greeted us pleasantly. "Good evening. Table for two?"

"Yes, thank you," I said.

"Smoking or nonsmoking?" he asked.

"Nonsmoking," I said. My first decision of the evening. And certainly not the last.

He said, "Would you prefer to dine indoors or out?"

"Indoors," I said.

"Very well," he said. "Would you prefer the main dining room, the enclosed patio, or our lovely solarium?"

"Gee, I don't know . . ."

He said, "I can give you a table with a lovely view in our lovely solarium."

I said, "I think your solarium would be lovely."

He asked, "Would you like a view overlooking the golf course, the majestic mountains to the north, or the sunset on our peaceful duck pond?"

I said, "Whatever you think." Let him make a decision for a change. He was younger than I was.

He gave us a table, and I have no idea what the view was because it was dark outside.

He left, and a waiter took over.

"Hi, my name is John, and I'll be your waiter this evening. Would you like to order or do you need a few minutes?"

"No, we'll order," I said. "I'll have a filet mignon with a baked potato."

He said, "Soup or salad?"

"Salad."

"We have a small dinner salad, a beet-and-goat-cheese salad, or an endive salad with baby shrimp."

I said, "I'll have the dinner salad."

"And your dressing?"

I didn't want to make another choice, so I said, "Whatever it comes with will be fine."

He wouldn't cut me any slack. "It comes with creamy Italian, Thousand Island, honey dijon—"

"Bring me one of those," I said.

"Which one?" he said. He was getting on my nerves. "The creamy Italian is our specialty. Would that be all right?"

"Yeah." I was curt. And I was done with civility.

He continued. "And your baked potato?"

I knew what was coming, and I wanted none of it. I said, "I just want the baked potato. I don't want anything on it. OK?"

"No sour cream?'

"No."

"No chives?"

"No." I said it louder.

"No butter?"

"I don't want anything on it. OK? I want it dry."

"Whatever you say, sir. Would you like the eight-ounce steak or the six-ounce steak?"

"Whatever."

"How would you like your steak? Rare? Medium rare? Medium well? Well done?"

I said, "You know, Johnny Boy, you're really starting to get me steamed."

"Which brings up the vegetables," he said. "We are offering steamed broccoli, creamed corn, sautéed zucchini. . ."

I'd had enough. I threw my napkin to the floor, stood up, and said, "How'd you like to settle this outside?"

He said, "If you wish, sir. Would you prefer the side alley, the street in front of the restaurant, or the parking lot out back?"

I said, "I prefer right here." I threw a punch and missed. He threw a punch and knocked me cold.

The maître d' rushed to my aid, chastised the waiter for fighting with a customer, and apologized to me.

I told him I was all right, but he said, "Can I bring you something, sir?"

I said, "Just a glass of water."

He said, "Right away, sir. Would you prefer imported mineral water, sparkling water, or simply club soda with a wedge of lime?"

So you can readily see that over the years, we've become disenchanted with deciding. However, the process is a bit more complicated than that. Let me explain:

Many self-help volumes promote decision making as the holy grail of leadership and success. Learn to make decisions, and you can have anything you want. Ralph Waldo Emerson said, "Once you make a decision, the universe conspires to make it happen." That's quite encouraging. You come to a conclusion—any conclusion—and the entire universe becomes your partner. You can't fail when you have everybody on your side and no one opposing you. It would be like watching a football game in which both teams decide to go on offense and no one is left to play defense. It might be a boring game, but there's no doubt that both teams will win.

Self-help deifies anyone who makes a decision. A CEO stands up at a company meeting and announces, "I've decided to expand our company by 35 percent this year." The listeners yell, "Huzzah, huzzah! What a great leader we have! He has made a decision!"

At another meeting across town, a CEO declares, "I've decided to downsize our company by 35 percent this year." The audience screams, "Huzzah, huzzah! What a great leader we have! He has made a decision!"

The four faces carved on Mount Rushmore are there because they were men who made decisions. Elvis Presley is "The King" because he made decisions (and he could sing a little). Meryl Streep is considered the consummate actor because she decided to play in *Kramer vs. Kramer, Sophie's Choice, Silkwood, Out of Africa, The Iron Lady*, and a whole bunch of other movies. She decided, and apparently the world conspired to make her talented.

Apparently, successful folks decide and the rest of us wander around willy-nilly, confused, unconcerned, and in general following the advice of Yogi Berra, who said, "When you come to a fork in the road, take it."

Here's the bottom line in this discussion: leaders make decisions. However, so does everyone else. All of us—losers, winners, don't-give-a-damners, rich, poor, young, old—make decisions. We make them every day and every minute. In fact, it's impossible not to make a decision.

Consider yourself in the morning. The alarm rings, summoning you to begin your workday. Do you pop out of bed eager to begin the day's toil, or do you hit the snooze button and sneak in five more minutes of carefree sleep? That's a decision.

When you do get out of bed, what's the first thing you do? Well, OK, there's probably no decision necessary there.

Now you begin to get ready for work. Do you wear the white shirt or the blue shirt? Decision. Do you wear the green tie or do you wear the purple tie? Your decision. Remember, too, that not making a decision is, in fact, making a decision.

Do you put on a pot of coffee, or will you stop at a café along the way and pick up a cup to go? Decision.

You've only been awake for ten minutes or so, and already you've been forced to resolve a fistful of dilemmas. Does this mean you're a leader? Is the entire world going to conspire to help you buy a cup of hot coffee? Does it indicate that Roosevelt and Lincoln should each move over a little to make room for your face to be carved into Mount Rushmore? No. It simply means that you're a guy who showed up for work shirtless (remember that not making a decision is, in fact, making a decision) but wearing either a green or a purple tie . . . or both (making both decisions is making a decision, too).

Decisions are no big deal. They're like breathing. We have to continue making them in order to get from one moment to the next. Leaders make them because they have no choice. Losers make them because we have no choice. Deciding is absolutely required.

Let's return to that moment when your alarm first sounded. You could either turn it off and hop out of bed or ignore it. You had to do one or the other. Admittedly, you did have a choice. However, you did not have the option of not choosing. If you didn't jump out of bed, you elected to stay there. If you didn't stay there, you elected to get out of bed. There was no way not to decide, so you don't get extra credit for that—despite what the self-help authors say.

Of course, there are good decisions and there are bad decisions. For instance, deciding to wear both the purple and the green tie to work would be an example of a bad decision. Not wearing a shirt with the purple and green ties is an example of a very bad decision.

So perhaps to be a leader and a success, you must make good decisions as opposed to bad decisions. Rather than simplifying things, though, this advice complicates it. Now in addition to making a decision, you must decide whether your decision is a good decision or a bad one. Ironically, that's an additional complication. Who decides whether your selection is a good one or a bad one? You know from watching the TV news broadcasts that people are usually divided. A politician proclaims the "wise" decision he has made. Some of the news channels glorify the choice. It exhibits courage, wisdom, compassion, brilliance, and a whole bunch of other complimentary nouns . . . and maybe a few laudatory adjectives to heighten the celebration. "Huzzah!" the commentators say, "Our leader has made a decision. And it is a good decision. He is courageous, wise, compassionate, brilliant, and all the other nouns and the accompanying adjectives, if any."

However, other news channels are not as impressed. They announce that this choice is cowardly, imbecilic, uncaring, dumb, and a whole bunch of other derogatory adjectives . . . with maybe a few contemptuous modifiers thrown in to highlight the stupidity of the choice.

Consequently, a good choice can also be a bad choice, depending on the news commentators you favor. And, of course, it almost goes without saying, which news commentators you watch is your decision.

We don't even need news commentators to make this point. Imagine a father who sacrifices to send his child to a renowned university. The kid is going to become a doctor, a lawyer, or some equally impressive and lucrative profession. The dad pays all the tuition, foots the bill for books, and supports his offspring throughout the journey. Finally, the youngster graduates and informs the family that he will now pursue a career as a rock musician. Try to guess whether the father thinks this is a good decision or a bad decision.

To further undermine the idea that decision making is the key to success, consider the idea that you need no qualifications to make a decision. This tale should illustrate that:

A couple went on vacation to a resort that permitted gambling. The husband asked his spouse how much she had lost at the gaming tables or the slot machines. She said, "I've lost about $40."

The husband was irritated. He said, "How can you lose that much money gambling? We struggled to afford this vacation, and we can't afford to toss away the money carelessly. You have to stop being so reckless." She asked, "How much have you lost?" He said, "About $2,500." She said, "How can you be so angry? You lost much more than I did." He said, "Yes, but I know what I'm doing."

The other ill-advised advice that self-help books offer is that leaders not only make decisions but stick by them. They are determined, fearless, resolute. They persevere in their choices until they yield results. Unfortunately, this is not leadership; it's lunacy.

Let's assume you want to drive from Los Angeles to San Francisco. Since you're not familiar with the route, you make a good choice and check the directions on your smartphone. Your phone correctly suggests that you take I-5 north, and in a little over six hours of driving time, you'll arrive in San Francisco.

But when you reach the entrance to the I-5 freeway, you make a bad decision and get on the I-5 freeway heading south. If, being the determined, fearless, resolute leader that the self-help books advise, you stubbornly stick with your decision, you will be driving for over six hours and never reach San Francisco. In fact, you'll drive through San Diego, California, and cross over into Tijuana, Mexico. You'll enjoy the scenery of Mexico until you reach Panama, the gateway to South America. After you pass through Panama, you'll travel along the mountains of Peru, down through Argentina. Eventually, you'll hit the southern tip of South America, where you'll probably run out of roadway.

According to the books, though, you'll be a wise and successful leader.

So what can we older folks learn from this advice? We know that decision making is an ongoing, never-ending, unavoidable process. We've been doing it for years and are either closer to our original goals or not. If we are, it has had nothing to do with our decision to make decisions. If we're not, it has nothing to do with our decision to make decisions.

We're not better leaders because we make decisions. That's like saying we make better leaders because we have a keen sense of smell. We smell whether we want to or not. Slice an onion, your eyes will water. Enter a hospital, and you'll immediately sense that it has a hospital smell. Frighten a skunk in your backyard, and you'll realize that you can no more control your sense of smell than you can control your decision making.

My advice is to ignore the traditional advice. Live your life in the moment. As Yogi Berra advised earlier, "When you come to a fork in the road, take it." Should you take the left path or the right? Decide. You may make a worthwhile choice, or you may make a defective one. If you make a good choice, be grateful. If you make a bad selection, be strong enough to reverse it. Regardless, you'll immediately be back to living in the present moment, which means that once again, you'll have a decision to make.

Above all, have some fun along the way. Don't take yourself or your decisions too seriously.

CHAPTER TWENTY-EIGHT

LEARN TO SAY "NO"

"What part of 'No' don't you understand?" —Anonymous

Self-help philosophies advocate positive traits and mentality. Confidence, courage, boldness, self-esteem, pluck, and der-ring-do are all imprinted on the banner of achievement. These are all commendable and beneficial in pursuing a goal. Some may even be indispensable. However, after reading this far, surely you've noticed that those of us who have had a few years of experience with the genre tend to be contrary—maybe even ornery.

Selective negativity is also not a bad characteristic to develop. There are times and situations in which, in order to advance, you should learn to say "No." The following are several of the circumstances where a positive "No" is recommended:

1. **Say "No" to wasting your talent.** Achieving any worthwhile goal requires planning, practice, perseverance, and effort. Often, the pursuit can become an obsession. It demands almost constant concentration on the objective and can be exhausting.

It's a long, challenging endeavor. All of your energy should be focused on the dream. Others, though, can distract you. They can ask you to donate your skills to some such event or another. Some of that is admirable—but not when it comes at the expense of your primary objective. So be generous when you can, but remember that most of your effort should go towards your advancement. Sometimes a "No" is a "Yes" to your best interests.

2. **Say "No" to other people's plans for you.** Often, other people take it on themselves to make plans for you. These are good folks who genuinely want you to succeed at whatever you desire. No, wait a minute. It could be that they want you to succeed at *whatever they desire.* Your parents could design the "ideal" future for you. Caring friends may offer help and advice—for what *they want you to do.* Teachers may advise you in one direction when you'd rather go in another. If their objectives are not your objectives, "No" is in order. Of course, it well could be that their suggestions coincide with your goals. Fine. Then go on and pursue away. But to proceed with confidence, courage, boldness, self-esteem, pluck, and all the other positives that the self-helpers advise, the trophy you're chasing should be the one you want to chase. Say "No" to all others.

3. **Say "No" to yourself.** *What? Is that a typo, or is that actually an admonition to refute your own thinking?* It does mean exactly what it says—there are times when you should say "No" to your own thoughts. *When?* you ask. Whenever you find yourself making a decision that should be left to the decision makers. "I won't try for this job because I know I'll never be hired." "I won't send this novel in to the publisher because these types of stories aren't selling this year." "I won't ask that girl out because women as pretty as her don't date guys like me." Notice in all of these examples that *you're* deciding when you should be letting

the person who will be making the decision decide. Maybe this company won't hire you. Maybe the publisher won't give you a contract for this book you've written. Maybe this young lady will find a way to turn down your polite proposal. But let these folks make the decision. If you make it for them, you'll never give them the opportunity to say "Yes" instead of "No." Whenever you're tempted to become the decision maker, tell yourself "No." Then go ahead and give it a try.

4. **Say "No" to evil.** There was a humorous placard a few years back that read, "Everything I like is illegal, immoral, or fattening." The funny implication was that as tempting as whatever you sought would appear, you had to reject it. You couldn't condone anything that was illegal or immoral. And, of course, fattening was simply out of the question. Some things are just wrong. Yes, there may be ways to obtain your objective, but if they're not proper, you must say "No" to them. The self-help philosophy convinces us that there are ways to achieve your goals legally and properly. We must stay within those guidelines.

5. **Say "No" to money.** *Whoa! Hold on! What's wrong with pursuing money?* Actually, nothing. Financial gain is a worthwhile pursuit. For some, it is the primary goal. Many people embrace self-help principles because they can lead to riches. However, there are often other considerations involved in these decisions. The "No" recommended here is to considering money as the overriding factor. Consider all the pertinent elements in making a decision, with money being only one of them. If attaining the money is not the wisest choice, you should say "No."

6. **Say "No" to any gain at another's expense.** Often, seeking achievement is a competitive endeavor. Only one person can win the race. So in a sense, your success contributes to another's disappointment. That's the way the game is played, and we all should accept those ground rules. However, to destroy

another's chance to attain his or her objective in order to guarantee yours is not acceptable. Go for the prize with gusto, but be fair in allowing your competitors the same opportunity you have. Say "No" to anything that wrongfully deprives them of that.

7. **Say "No" to the easy way out.** Responsible self-help literature doesn't hide the fact that pursuing a goal requires planning, practice, and effort. The books do try to make your achievement easier by applying their ideas, but they can never eliminate the struggle totally. You should be wary of trying to eliminate the exertion, too. Be wary of unnatural, too-good-to-be-true shortcuts. The easy way out may be the most tempting, but it's not always the most beneficial. Don't be too ready to avoid the hard work. Sometimes, it's the hard work that renders the goal reachable.

8. **Say "No" to fear.** As this book has noted many times, William Shakespeare made this point most eloquently. In his play *Measure for Measure,* his character Lucio says, "Our doubts are traitors and make us lose the good we oft might win by fearing to attempt." Once we make a decision to abandon a quest based on fear, we forfeit any good that might have resulted from a courageous attempt. Fear can be a benefit when it prompts caution. It's not wise to be foolhardy. However, basing a decision on fear alone often is foolhardy. If you're faced with a decision dependent on fear or boldness, say "No" to fear. As Shakespeare counsels, think of the good you oft might win.

9. **Say "No" to avoiding risks.** No worthwhile pursuit is ever risk-free. Generally, there comes a time when you have to make up your mind—do it or don't. Harry Truman once said, "If you can't stand the heat, get out of the kitchen." There's going to be some heat involved in any achievement you seek. The risk can make it seem not worth the attempt, but it may be the risk that

makes the goal that much more desirable. Some wise person once said, "If it were easy, everybody would do it." Keep that thought in mind when you face a challenging decision, and say "No" to avoiding the risk.

10. **Say "No" to becoming someone else.** Pursuing a goal is a journey. It would be ideal if you are the same person at the end of the trip as you are at the beginning. We sometimes try to mold ourselves to the image that people expect of us. We sacrifice some of what we are in hopes of becoming what they might want us to be. Why not be yourself and let the others adjust to that? You're probably the best person in the world at being you. What good is reaching a goal if you're not the person who deserves that reward? Besides, when you try to mold yourself to someone else's image of you, you're only guessing at what that image is. You don't know. It's safer to be yourself.

11. **Say "No" to surrendering control.** The television industry is noted for changing concepts drastically but gradually. Authors can go to a meeting with a brilliant, unique premise that they are eager to produce. The executives they meet with love the idea. However, they ask for a minor change. The author wants to sell the idea, so she agrees. Then the execs ask for a few more "minor" changes. The author again accepts those suggestions. After a few more sessions, the brilliant, unique notion is gradually transformed into a pedestrian, predictable, boilerplate sitcom that the author no longer wants to write but must. That could possibly happen with the goal you're pursuing. You might allow others to transform it into a goal you no longer are exuberant about. Any goal you chase should be one that you consider worth chasing. You should be totally in command. Say "No" to any thought of surrendering your control.

12. **Say "No" to hesitation or procrastination.** Opportunity doesn't knock just once, but it's not going to keep banging your

door down if you don't respond. It's wise to explore any promising occasions that present themselves. If you're confident and prepared, you should take advantage. To delay because of fear or uncertainty can be costly. Do consider the opportunity, and if it proves viable, say "No" to hesitation or procrastination.

13. **Say "No" to rushing ahead without proper preparation.** Sure, we just talked about acting without delay when an opportunity arises. Now we're suggesting that you not rush in blindly. To pass up a worthwhile chance can be disastrous. However, taking on an assignment that you're not prepared for can be just as devastating. As you pursue your goal, you should be ready and able to meet its demands. Are you ready? Can you fulfill the obligations? You are the one who must answer that honestly. If you sincerely feel you need more training or more experience, then take the time to get it. This should be an honest evaluation on your part, though. Keep in mind once again Shakespeare's warning that "our doubts are traitors and make us lose the good we oft might win by fearing to attempt." Be bold enough to try, but also be courageous and wise enough to know when you're not yet ready.

14. **Say "No" to cheating.** All of your accomplishments should be attained according to the rules and regulations. You know what's right and proper. Say "No" to anything that isn't.

15. **Say "No" to discourtesy.** Someone once advised, "Be nice to the people you meet on the way up the ladder of success. You may meet the same people on the way down." That's sort of a negative take on the admonition, but it's worth noting. A more positive outlook may be "Be nice to the people you meet on the way up the ladder of success. They may be the very people who can help you move up that ladder more quickly." Congeniality, cooperation, and consideration are valid tools in pursuing any goal. And this applies to all of the people you deal with, from

GENE PERRET   225

the person who answers your first phone call to the CEO who eventually will make the momentous decisions about your fate.

16. **Say "No" to superiority.** As you reach more and more plateaus on your achievement journey, you'll grow in stature. As things work out, you'll become more and more renowned, more and more respected. That's commendable—provided you carry it well. One gentleman talked quite eloquently about this phenomenon. He was an extraordinarily wealthy man who attended some gala in a chauffeur-driven limousine. Some reporter commented on that. He said, "Boy, a chauffeur-driven limousine. That's class." The man corrected him. He said, "No, a chauffeur-driven limousine is not class. That's the accoutrements of class. Real class is how you treat your chauffeur." So when you're tempted to be a bit highfalutin, say "No" to it.

17. **Say "No" to bad advice.** One thing you'll never be short of on your journey towards your goal is advice. Many people who have no idea where you're going will tell you the best way to get there. You'll get good advice, and you'll get bad advice. Part of your challenge will be to decide which is which. A wise philosopher, Conway Twitty, once said, "Listen to advice, but follow your heart." Another sage, Joan Rivers, offered, "Don't follow any advice, no matter how good, until you feel as deeply in your spirit as you think in your mind that the counsel is wise." Those are two entertainers who reached their goals, telling us quite articulately to say "No" to bad advice.

18. **Say "No" to complacency.** Once, I enrolled my grandson in a tennis camp for youngsters. He was only about six years old at the time. I watched him and his colleagues flail at the ball and hit it into the net, over the fence, and occasionally into the opposite court where it should have gone. After ten weeks of this, the camp offered a follow-up series of lessons. I asked my grandson if he wanted to be part of the new class. He said, "No,

I know all there is to know about tennis now." Often, we can deceive ourselves into believing the same thing. In our quest for achievement, we pass through several plateaus. It's easy to mistake a plateau for the ultimate goal. When you're tempted to say "I've done what I set out to do. I can now rest on my laurels," instead say "No" to that complacency. Keep grinding.

19. **Say "No" to rejection and disappointment.** There are setbacks on any road to success. Not every manuscript you submit will be published. Not every job you apply for will be yours. Not every contest you enter will declare you the winner. That's all part of the journey. You must recognize that some rejection is justified. You may not be as accomplished as you think. That's the time when you should take inventory of yourself, your determination, and your talent. Rather than discourage you, it should inspire you to work harder and prepare better so that eventually the rejection will turn to acceptance. There's a saying you've surely heard: "If at first you don't succeed, try, try again." It doesn't say "If at first you don't succeed, aw, forget about it."

20. **Say "No" to unhealthy habits.** Athletes know the benefits of being in condition for the competition. They devote much time to building endurance and stamina. They know the value of good training habits. We're all like athletes competing for the prize. Any pursuit we undertake has demands, and we should always be in condition to stand up under those requirements. What we eat and drink and how we exercise affect our performance. With that in mind, we should learn to say "No" to bad habits. Remember, the hare probably would have won the contest against the tortoise if he had gotten a little more sleep the night before the race.

So, yes, approach your quest with positive thoughts, with confidence, and with determination. But learn when to say "Yes" and when to say "No" if you want to reach the finish line.

CONCLUSION

"Be yourself. Everyone else is already taken." —Oscar Wilde

D o we get better with age? Let me give you an idea of how we improve over the years. A few years ago, my granddaughter was about five or six years old, and she said to me, "Pop-pop, you have books and you know some of the people in the movies and on TV. Pop-pop, you're famous."

Today she's approaching twenty years of age. She says to me, "Pop-pop, you're cute."

So folks, we don't get better or wiser: we get cuter.

We've just run through a gamut of self-help advice. The philosophy has been around for years, and it has done wonders for many people. Bless them. They worked hard to apply the principles, and it paid rewards. Good for them.

Not so good for us older folks, though. We didn't pay proper attention when we should have. It's not the fault of the self-help gurus. It's our fault. We were young and foolish. We still are, except for the "young" part. We're not wiser than the younger folks. We just lord it over them because we've been dumb longer than they have.

Much of the advice the self-help authors offer is valid, but we reject it. Some of it we can't do. Physically, we're no longer equipped. It's kind of like trying to become a gymnast at the age of eighty-seven.

Some of it we just can't be bothered with. We're older. We're allowed to pick and choose our protocols, and many of them we flat out reject.

Some of their advice we reject but wish our friends would follow.

Is improvement impossible for us? I hope not, and I'm sure you do, too.

One surefire path to success in any field is to be good at what you do and keep getting better at it. Eventually, you reach excellence; then you can write your own ticket.

So self-improvement for us older folks is rather simple. We just have to be a better person tomorrow than we are today. Use any self-help philosophy or advice that makes you even a tiny bit better.

Keep being yourself, but just a bit better each day. Try it . . . it works.

ABOUT THE AUTHOR

GENE PERRET used many self-help principles in building several successful careers. He wrote on a number of top-rated television shows and was head writer for Bob Hope and Phyllis Diller for almost three decades. As part of *The Carol Burnett Show* writing staff, he earned three Emmy Awards. Gene produced and was head writer for TV shows such as *Three's Company, Welcome Back Kotter,* and Tim Conway's variety show.

Gene has written numerous books on comedy writing, several of which have been considered textbook quality and used in several colleges.

He's also written articles for various magazines, among them *Reader's Digest, McCall's,* and *Toastmaster.* Gene has written a monthly humor column for *Arizona Highways* for ten years.

Today he plays golf and guitar, both poorly, and plans to spend the rest of his days learning how to use the smartphone his children bought him for Christmas.

ABOUT FAMILIUS

Welcome to a place where parents are celebrated, not compared. Where heart is at the center of our families, and family at the center of our homes. Where boo-boos are still kissed, cake beaters are still licked, and mistakes are still okay. Welcome to a place where books—and family—are beautiful. Familius: a book publisher dedicated to helping families be happy.

VISIT OUR WEBSITE: WWW.FAMILIUS.COM

Our website is a different kind of place. Get inspired, read articles, discover books, watch videos, connect with our family experts, download books and apps and audiobooks, and along the way, discover how values and happy family life go together.

JOIN OUR FAMILY

There are lots of ways to connect with us! Subscribe to our newsletters at www.familius.com to receive uplifting daily inspiration, essays from our Pater Familius, a free ebook every month, and the first word on special discounts and Familius news.

BECOME AN EXPERT

Familius authors and other established writers interested in helping families be happy are invited to join our family and contribute online content. If you have something important to say on the family, join our expert community by applying at:

www.familius.com/apply-to-become-a-familius-expert

GET BULK DISCOUNTS

If you feel a few friends and family might benefit from what you've read, let us know and we'll be happy to provide you with quantity discounts. Simply email us at orders@familius.com.

Website: www.familius.com

Facebook: www.facebook.com/paterfamilius

Twitter: @familiustalk, @paterfamilius1

Pinterest: www.pinterest.com/familius

The most important work you ever do will be within the walls of your own home.

CPSIA information can be obtained
at www.ICGtesting.com
Printed in the USA
FSOW01n2358050416
18857FS